The Heart of Social Psychology

The Heart of Social Psychology

A Backstage View of a Passionate Science
Second Edition

by

ARTHUR ARON
University of California, Santa Cruz
ELAINE N. ARON

Lexington Books

D.C. Heath and Company · Lexington, Massachusetts · Toronto

Library of Congress Cataloging-in-Publication Data

Aron, Arthur.
The heart of social psychology : a backstage view of a passionate science / by Arthur Aron, Elaine N. Aron.—2nd ed.
p. cm.
Includes index.
ISBN 0–669–21180–X (alk. paper).—ISBN 0–669–21144–3 (pbk. : alk. paper)
1. Social psychology. I. Aron, Elaine. II. Title.
HM251.A788 1989
302—dc19
89–2431
CIP

Published simultaneously in Canada
Printed in the United States of America
Casebound International Standard Book Number: 0–669–21180–X
Paperbound International Standard Book Number: 0–669–21144–3
Library of Congress Catalog Card Number: 89–2431

The paper used in this publication meets the minimum requirements of American National Standard for Information Sciences—Permanence of Paper for Printed Library Materials, ANSI Z39.48–1984.

∞™

Year and number of this printing:

92 10 9 8 7 6 5 4 3

Contents

Introduction

SOCIAL psychology is a big, busy discipline. But deep at its center there is a heart. A passionate heart. This heart only appears between the lines in social psychology textbooks and research articles. But it is there, in its traditions, in its researchers, in their relationships. The purpose of this book is to reveal that heart, to take you backstage and let you see what a science feels like to those who have devoted their lives to it. While we are there, we would like to give you some informal descriptions of social psychology's major findings, for these are also part of its heart.

The Heart of Social Psychology began as a personal account, based on our impressions over the years. But we saw right away that we needed to buttress our impressions with the experiences of others, and so we looked for more data. That is, like most work in social psychology, the project developed into something bigger, more inclusive, and more social.

First we read: Kurt Lewin's biography, Fritz Heider's autobiography, and the delightful contributions by social psychologists to Edwin Boring and Gardner Lindzey's *A History of Psychology in Autobiography.* Next were Richard Evans's interviews in *The Making of Social Psychology* and David Cohen's in *Psychologists on Psychology,* plus various histories of the field, such as Gordon Allport's classic essay in the *Handbook of Social Psychology,* Ivan Steiner's chapter in *The First Century of Experimental Psychology,* several articles by Dorwin Cartwright, and Leon Festinger's volume of *Retrospectives on Social Psychology.* Then there was the "crisis" literature from the seventies, when social psychologists wrote long, fervent articles to one another about where social psychology should be going. And there were also introductions to books, parentheses and asides in articles and chapters, and the *American Psychologist* award presentations and obituaries, all of which proved useful too.

It occurred to us, however, that we ought to check our hypotheses about the field with some of our friends who are social psychologists. So we sat and talked with them, took a few notes, and began to see that we needed to change strategy again. We needed their ideas. Dorwin Cartwright (1979) pointed out a decade ago that 90 percent of all the people who have ever been social psychologists were still alive. And the figure should be even higher today, as the field is still rapidly expanding. *They* are the field. The books and the histories are important only in showing how these living social psychologists developed as they have.

We started out chatting with them and taking sketchy notes, but soon we wanted to save everything on a tape recorder. Similarly, at first we'd ask whatever came to mind, but over the fifty or so interviews a six-page interview protocol evolved. The best questions, as it turned out, were "How did you get into social psychology?"; "When teaching social psychology, is there any overarching theme you try to convey, over and above the specific findings, methods, and theories of the field?"; "Of all the things you do in your daily life as a social psychologist, what is the most rewarding?"; "Where do you see social psychology going in the future?"; and "What would you tell someone who is considering becoming a social psychologist?"

The questioning was often personal and even pushy: For example, "But *why* is that meaningful to you?" Still, our respondents were uniformly friendly, helpful, and even enthusiastic about the project. In Ellen Berscheid's opinion, social psychologists are unusually "nice people." From our experience we would certainly agree.

Each interview lasted about an hour. When possible, the interviews were in person—though often at odd times and locales. We met Phil Zimbardo after he gave a talk at the Palo Alto Veterans Administration hospital. We wandered around together for a half-hour, looking for the canteen to have a soft drink; the tape is full of hospital announcements punctuating Phil's wonderful stories. The interview with Lee Ross was conducted outside, at a fish-and-chips restaurant. The interview with Elliot Aronson was carried on over a breakfast we purchased with a two-for-one coupon at a Santa Cruz coffeehouse. But the vast majority of interviews were conducted over the telephone.[1]

We readily admit that the people we chose to interview were not a systematically representative sample of anything. They were simply some social psychologists who usually but not always (a) were our friends; (b) lived near us; (c) had conducted a study we were discussing in the book; (d) had been suggested to us by others; (e) were obviously eminent; or (f) were people we had always wanted to meet.

If persons were *not* interviewed whom readers might have expected us to interview, these were probably persons (a) we could not reach on the phone; (b) who had written autobiographies or had been interviewed at length in some other published source; (c) we did not think of; or (d) whose phone numbers were stuck in the wrong folder.

We found these interviews delightful and inspiring. We are grateful to those we did talk with, for their time and willingness to cooperate. Interviewed were Elliot Aronson, John Arrowood, Solomon Asch, Daryl Bem, Jerry Burger, Ellen Berscheid, Marilyn Brewer, Morton Deutsch, Donald Dutton, Russel Fazio, J. B. Gilmore, William Graziano, Anthony Greenwald, O. J. Harvey, Elaine Hatfield, Harold Kelley, Herbert Kellman, Lee Ross, Edward Sampson, Theodore Sarbin, Stanley Schachter, Muzafer Sherif, Jerry Singer, Elizabeth Tanke, Dalmas Taylor, Abraham Tesser, John Touhey, and Philip Zimbardo. And for this second edition, Carl Backman, Margaret Clark, Steve Duck, Alice Eagley, Susan Fiske, Craig Haney, Edward E. Jones, Bibb

[1]We used state-of-the-art technology and controlled laboratory conditions for our first-edition interviews: A cheap Radio Shack microphone hung from a desk lamp so that it dangled an inch above our speakerphone. Alas, our phone had "call waiting," and so some interviews were interrupted by urgent calls from our teenage son. Hal Kelley graciously accommodated three such interruptions in a half-hour. But by the second edition, technology had advanced to the point that we could record the interviews on our answering machine. And our son had advanced to the point of being away at college.

Latane, George McCall, David Myers, Tom Pettigrew, Anthony Pratkanis, Harry Reis, Deborah Richardson, Judith Schwartz, Phillip Shaver, M. Brewster Smith, Gregory White, and Robert Zajonc.

As a result of gathering all this information, we began to think of social psychologists in terms of a set of characteristics, and these traits became our eventual chapter topics: Most social psychologists evidence chutzpah, an insistence on the reality of social influence and cognitions, a personal awareness of that reality, a love of playful research and intricate theory, and a concern for the world. Certainly not every, and possibly not any one, social psychologist exhibits all these characteristics. But each quality is typical of many in this very heterogeneous field. Our set of characteristics also rang a bell for those we talked with, seeming typical of others they knew. Perhaps what we have described is a sort of "paradigm case" of a social psychologist, in the sense of the descriptive psychology employed by Keith Davis and his associates.

But this little book was never intended to be a piece of research. At its best, it may be a quasi survey (or perhaps only quasi literature). Our hope was simply that these chapters would seem about right to our colleagues, perhaps verbalizing some things they hadn't thought about and helping their students to appreciate the discipline, culture, and joy behind the formal course offerings. Maybe this book will even satisfy the occasional curiosity of the general public, especially at those times when this field slips momentarily into journalistic prominence. We'd like that.

Since you may have noticed that this is a second edition, we ought now to explain what is new about it. Our methods stayed the same but yielded fresh insights. We read more—particularly some of the new scholarship on the history of the field—and we interviewed nineteen more of our fellow social psychologists. The rewriting of this book also had the benefit of its having been used for three years to liven up social science courses. Three fellow social psychologists in particular—Elliot Aronson, David Myers, and Gregory White—gave us helpful suggestions based on their use of the first edition. We are also grateful to Anthony Pratkanis and Judy Schwartz, who were kind enough to read the draft of this second edition. Of course, none of our colleagues would agree with everything we have ended up saying. Nor should they. This is, after all, still a personal sort of book.

All of this input has brought about changes as well as additions. Our entire orientation as authors has subtly shifted from participant-observer storytellers to backstage tour guides. And our description of the field has honed in a little more sharply on what we call the "passionate" character of our science. Both these developments are reflected in the new subtitle.

Yet another subtle change results from our realization that the book is being read mainly by students—not only in social psychology classes but in introductory and history of psychology courses and in "sociological social psychology" classes, as an introduction to the "psychological" side of the field. While we still hope the book will find its way beyond the classroom, we have tried to shape this edition to help ease students' anxiety about what they have to study for an exam. (If you are a student, the answer is this: Learn the studies and theories and perhaps the basic theme of each chapter. The quotations from working social psychologists are there to make the ideas vivid, not to be learned!) We hope this new edition will continue to serve students and professors well.

But the most important changes are probably the most subtle of all—changes that reflect the developments of the past three years and our perception of them; changes that have created a slight reframing of the field as a bit more mature, a bit more professional, a bit more diverse. Lewin's students—and most of his students' students—are older than Lewin when he died, and the field has been gradually institutionalizing and professionalizing many of its passionate traits.

But don't lose heart! This greater solidity has poised the field for its greatest potential yet. And, it seems to us, social psychology is still the boldest of the sciences. Intense in its desire for knowledge. Delighted by the process of discovery.

Above all, whatever changes this new edition reflects, we hope we have successfully resisted the forces of "maturity" that so often make second editions more "acceptable," blander versions of the original. Our goal has been to retain what many have told us they found most engaging: this book's direct, unabashed sharing of the true heart of social psychology.

1

Chutzpah

Social Psychology Takes on the Big Issues

CHUTZPAH is a Yiddish word meaning the guts to stick your neck out, perhaps even a little *too* far out, and take on something really big. Social psychologists abound in chutzpah, confidently believing that any social question worth debating is worth testing rigorously, if possible with an experiment that sorts out the underlying causes. No area of human concern, from the most pressing practical problems to the most long-standing philosophical issues, is beyond the reach of some determined social psychologist.

A prime example (among hundreds) is Stanley Schachter. So far in his prolific and audacious career, he has studied why people want to be with others, how people know what they feel, what makes people overweight, why people commit crimes, and why people smoke. All these areas have stymied other researchers and the public for years. But whatever the project, in each case Schachter quickly makes breakthroughs. "There's no such thing as a tough area," Schachter has said. "An area's only tough if you don't have an idea" (quoted in Evans, 1976, p. 166). When pressed, Schachter admitted that

> it's hard to talk about some of these things without sounding pompous. But if I were forced to give advice, I'd say, get problem-

> oriented, follow your nose and go where problems lead you. Then if something opens up that's interesting and that requires techniques and knowledge with which you're unfamiliar, learn them. (p. 168)

It's that simple when you have chutzpah.

The same sentiment was expressed by Robert Zajonc—an eminent social psychologist especially admired for his gutsiness by many of the social psychologists we interviewed for this book. Over the years, Zajonc has been responsible for a series of breakthrough theories and unexpected experimental results, ranging from the arousing effects on the individual of working in the presence of others to long-term changes in the appearance of married partners.

When we asked Zajonc about social psychology, his attitude was like Schachter's. Zajonc said:

> All problems are solvable. It is simply a matter of finding the methods. . . . Two weeks before the Wright brothers took off from Kitty Hawk, a man named Simon Newcomb published in *Science* a definitive article showing that it's absolutely impossible to build a machine heavier than air that would fly. So if you did a meta-analysis of all empirical research done before the Wright brothers, the conclusion would be it's pointless. Give up. . . . [But with any problem,] it's just a matter of being clever enough, or lucky enough, to formulate it in a way that makes it solvable.

Kurt Lewin—Chutzpah versus Hitler

Stanley Schachter was first a student of Kurt Lewin, whom many consider the founder of modern social psychology. Later Schachter was a student of one of Lewin's famous students, Leon Festinger. Robert Zajonc was a student of Lewin's heir apparent, Desmond Cartwright. Through Schachter, Festinger, Cartwright, and numerous others, Kurt Lewin was the single greatest influence on social psychology—"the giant," according to another eminent pioneer in the field, Theodore Newcomb (quoted in Hilgard, 1987, p. 604). Nearly every major trend in social psychology—group dynamics, cognitive dissonance, attribution theory—has been primarily developed by a student or close associate of Kurt Lewin. After Lewin's death in 1947, the great learning psychologist Edward Tolman wrote:

> Freud, the clinician, and Lewin, the experimentalist, these are the two men who will always be remembered because of the fact that their contrasting but complementary insights first made of psychology a science which was applicable both to real individuals and to real society. (1948, p. 26)

Yet Lewin has hardly achieved the psychic demigod status of Freud. Lewin's theory is no longer widely used in social psychology, and his name appears on only a few research studies. So what was his great influence?

Lewin role-modeled chutzpah (and most of the other qualities of social psychology discussed in this book).

And when Lewin role-modeled something, it stuck. He has been described as "the most charismatic psychologist of his generation" (Hilgard, 1987, p. 588). Or, as Brewster Smith put it, "he had this knack of catalyzing excitement around himself."

Lewin came to America—to Iowa, the heartland—in the mid-1930s. He was fleeing Hitler, and while Lewin was a gentle person, he could also be stubborn. Loving democracy deeply, he set out to attack tyranny the best way he knew, through the new science of social psychology.

Lewin's commitment to democracy was more than abstract political ideology. In contrast to Freud, his very style of *doing* science was democratic. As we said, Lewin's influence was not mainly from his own personal theories or research. It wasn't even from his lectures. It was from his Quasselstrippe (a German word roughly meaning "bull session"), where he sat around chatting with his students and playing with ideas. As their organizer and informal leader, he showed consistent respect and warmth. Whether he was listening to an undergraduate or an eminent colleague, everyone's ideas received a hearing. Lewin was enormously creative, but most important he facilitated creativity in those around him, through his enthusiastic and democratic intellectual leadership.[1]

While Lewin was noted for his good humor, he was vehement on one subject. That, of course, was democracy. Robert Sears, a well-known developmental theorist and colleague of Lewin's at the University of Iowa, commented about Lewin, "The autocratic way he insisted on democracy was a little spectacular. . . . There was nothing to criticize—but one could not help noticing the fire and the emphasis" (quoted in Marrow, 1969, p. 127).

With such fire, it was not surprising that when one of Lewin's new graduate students, Ronald Lippitt, asked about studying the effect of different kinds of leadership structures, Lewin immediately abandoned his other research plans and plunged into the idea.[2] Together with Lippitt, Lewin constructed an ingenious series of experiments to compare scientifically the effects of autocratic versus democratic leadership.

It was a revolutionary idea to take this age-old question of practical affairs and social philosophy and subject it to rigorous scientific scrutiny. Lewin was adamant, however, that all life was the domain of the new science of social psychology. Nothing need be left to speculation and argument. Experimental research would solve the perennial problems of humankind.

The experiment itself was elegantly simple. The subjects were eleven-year-old boys who had volunteered to participate. The researchers organized them into several "clubs" of five boys each, each group a similar composite of personalities (based on teachers' assessments). The clubs chose such names as "Sher-

[1]Everyone we have spoken with who knew Lewin remarked on his enthusiasm: "He sparkled," as one put it. This enthusiasm was so contagious that when Lewin first visited the United States in 1929, when he still could speak only German, he developed a following that included some who could not understand a word of his talks. They were just taken by the man!

[2]Lewin had a warm, easy relationship with everyone around him, including his graduate students. They, in the great American tradition, returned his affection in a variety of ways—including practical jokes. Lippitt told Brewster Smith (an eminent social psychologist, of a later era) the following story: At Iowa, Lewin's graduate students were helping him to get acculturated to the strange ways of America, and they also liked to tease him. So in the process of teaching him American slang, they explained to him that when you really agree with something a person has said, you say, "You sure slobbered a bibful"—a compliment the innocent Lewin proceeded to pay an important colleague during a major scientific presentation.

lock Holmes," "Dick Tracy," "Secret Agents," and "Charlie Chan." Each club was assigned an adult leader to help it carry out its crafts, games, and so forth over the next twenty weeks of meetings. To assess what went on in the groups, during each meeting several researchers observed. The boys and their parents were also interviewed later about the groups. The groups differed in only one respect—the behavior of the adult leaders.

Initially the leaders adopted one of two styles. One was *autocratic,* in which the leader took charge of every aspect of the tasks, kept the boys in the dark about the next step, and generally maintained complete authority at all times. The other was *democratic,* in which the leader encouraged group discussion and decision making and saw that during each step of an activity the boys were aware of that step's purpose in achieving the activity's overall goal.

Later, when Ralph White came to Iowa as a postdoctoral fellow in political science, he could not resist joining the social psychologists' research team. When White attempted to play the democratic leader, however, Lippitt and Lewin noted that his version of the democratic leader was quite different from the others'. Rather than changing White's approach to the role, Lewin realized that White was really demonstrating a third important leader type: *laissez-faire,* in which the leader plays a completely passive role, allowing members to do as they please and interfering as little as possible.

Thus, in its final form the study compared three leadership styles and the social climates surrounding them (Lewin, Lippitt, & White, 1939; Lippitt & White, 1947). Great care was taken to make the leaders' behaviors similar in all other ways—for example, in how much joking and kindness they expressed. Each club experienced more than one kind of leader, in a systematic rotation.

The result was clear. Under autocratic leadership, the groups' behaviors fell into one of two general styles: passive and dependent or hostile and resistant. Either way, the autocratic groups' members were less satisfied and less friendly with one another in and out of the groups.

With democratic leadership, there was the greatest independence, the least discontent, and the most friendliness in and out of the group. Moreover, during activities members cooperated more and concentrated more on getting their task done.

The laissez-faire groups were closer to the democratic than the autocratic groups in many ways, except that the members were considerably more apathetic and less work-oriented.

Perhaps the most interesting differences emerged during "test episodes." In one, the experimenters arranged for the leader to come late. On their own, the democratic groups worked well; the authoritarian groups simply stopped doing much of anything; and the laissez-faire groups were active but not very effective in their activities.

In another test episode the experimenters sent in a stranger (a "janitor" or "electrician") while the leader was out, to criticize the group and its members. The authoritarian groups responded with much more hostility, perhaps showing a scapegoating effect.

Almost all the boys preferred the periods in which they had a democratic leader, but the transitions were difficult for most, especially from autocratic to democratic or laissez-faire.

Lewin was not shy about drawing conclusions:

> On the whole, I think that there is ample proof that the difference in behavior in autocratic and democratic situations is not a result of differences in the individuals. There have been few experiences for me as impressive as seeing the expression on children's faces during the first day under an autocratic leader. The group that had formerly been friendly, open, cooperative, and full of life, became within a short half-hour a rather apathetic-looking gathering without initiative. The change from autocracy to democracy seemed to take somewhat more time than that from democracy to autocracy. Autocracy is imposed on the individual. Democracy he has to learn! (1939, p. 31)

Muzafer Sherif Tackles the Problem of War and Peace

Of course, Lewin was not the only source of chutzpah for social psychology. Another pioneer was Muzafer Sherif, who studied under Gardner Murphy at Columbia University. Murphy was a contemporary of Lewin's; in 1935 he wrote (with Lois Murphy) the first modern social psychology text. Later, Gardner Murphy said that social psychology started out as a "relatively well-behaved junior sib among the big boys and girls [of mainstream psychology] who had been around longer and knew better how to accommodate to the academic giants" (1965, p. 24). But, he noted, "Some of the creative people refused to work within the psychology that was standard for their era. Think of the rebels like Lewin, Sherif, and Moreno" (p. 24).

One must also think of Murphy himself, who was just as confident as Lewin that no human folly would dare to persist once psychology had identified what needed to be done. And so Murphy passed all this social psychology chutzpah on to his students, including Muzafer Sherif, a young graduate student from Turkey who had come to America to study psychology.[3] (You'll learn all about Sherif's dramatic decision to study social psychology in chapter 7.)

Sherif challenged the conventional methods of measuring attitudes and then conducted one of the first studies experimentally delineating the process of the formation of social norms (Sherif, 1935). But of all his contributions, the chutzpahs shows through most in a series of three "summer camp" studies (Sherif, Harvey, White, Hood, & Sherif, 1961), culminating in the study subtitled *The Robber's Cave Experiment.* This is the study that Sherif told us was, among all his works, "closest to my heart."

At Robber's Cave, Oklahoma, Sherif and his students, O.J. Harvey, B.J. White, and W.E. Hood, modestly set out to study the formation of culture, the causes of intergroup conflict, and the resolution of intergroup enmity. (The results were then written up by Sherif's wife, the independently famous social psychologist Carolyn Wood Sherif.) Thus, in a single study, Sherif and company attacked the issues of what creates a society and what causes war and peace.

During the summer of 1954, a number of upper-middle-class, eleven- and twelve-year-old boys were invited to attend "a spe-

[3]Murphy continued to be an important figure in psychology but mainly in the area of personality theory and research.

cial summer camp" at Robber's Cave.[4] When they arrived, before they even saw each other, they were randomly divided into two groups and sent to different parts of the large campground. For the first few days, each group was not even aware of the other's existence. Nevertheless, by the second week loyalties were strong. Each group had named itself, and both the Eagles and the Rattlers had developed leaders and informal social rules.

As soon as the two groups did hear about each other, each began to challenge the other to competitions. The researchers added fuel to this inherent competitive spark by bringing the two groups together to play team games, including very hard fought tugs-of-war. In all these competitions the winning group received a prize and the loser nothing.

The researchers used every opportunity to increase the losers' frustration. One technique, developed at a similar camp a previous summer, was to give a party after a competition to "let bygones be bygones." The experimenters deliberately arranged for half the refreshments to be "delectable and whole," while the other half were "crushed and unappetizing." One group was brought to the party just earlier enough to allow its members to select, naturally, all the delectable appetizers. When the other group arrived, they were faced with the unappealing leftovers and the spectacle of plates full of good stuff on the laps of their enemies. The late group was hardly pacified by this turn of events.

Even without this encouragement, the groups had developed an "in-group versus out-group" mentality. Each group called the members of the other group names and considered them inferior. On a questionnaire, the vast majority of both groups rated their own members as "brave," "tough," and "friendly" and rated the other group's as "sneaky," "smart-alecks," and "stinkers."

---

[4]One commentator (MacKinnon, 1949) pointed out that Lewin, and presumably Sherif, worked with children for the same reason that learning psychologists work with rats: They are simpler organisms. (One wonders how many children these researchers knew intimately.) That is, one can see the deeper principles without adult complications. But no doubt another reason was the one which now explains the use of sophomore college students: The kids were available, and they were willing or obliged to do what they were told.

But now came the next, too-human stage: war. Fights broke out, flags were stolen, raids undertaken, green apples hoarded for "ammunition." The group structures themselves became all too reminiscent of societies at war, with leadership assigned by the group to the toughest kids and with a great focus on attacks and the "enemy." In fact, the researchers had to intervene several times to avoid bloodshed.

Then began the most challenging part of the study. Having created this microcosm of an intolerant and warring world, Sherif and company set out to create peace. First they tried bringing opposing factions together to share pleasant activities. It didn't work; a joint banquet turned into a food fight.

Another idea was religious services emphasizing peacemaking:

> The topics were brotherly love, forgiveness of enemies, and cooperation. The boys arranged the services and were enthusiastic about the sermon. Upon solemnly departing from the ceremony, they returned within minutes to their concerns to defeat, avoid, or retaliate against the detested out-group. (Sherif & Sherif, 1969, pp. 254–55)

Yet another idea was conferences between the group leaders. But the staff didn't even try to arrange them, given the outcome of a spontaneous attempt of this kind during one of the early experiments:

> A high status [member of one group] went on his own initiative to the [other group's] cabin with the aim of negotiating better relationships. He was greeted by a hail of green apples, chased down the path, and derided. Upon returning to his own group, he received no sympathy. Despite his high status, he was rebuked for making the attempt, which was doomed to failure in the opinion of his fellow members. (p. 255)

So much for negotiations. In fact, with every attempt to resolve the conflict, whether initiated by the experimenters or the boys themselves, the hostility seemed only to increase. Indeed, in the first two summer-camp studies, the boys went home harboring a good deal of bad feeling against the opposing groups.

Fortunately for everyone, however, during the 1954 camping session at Robber's Cave the experimenters finally found a strategy that worked: They introduced *superordinate goals.* This was done by setting up a series of situations in which the two groups had to cooperate to attain a joint objective. For example, the camp food truck would not start (thanks to the researchers' surreptitious efforts) and all the boys had to pull together, literally, to get the truck going. Another time the water supply "accidentally" broke down and the boys had to work together to locate the problem along a mile of pipe.

Gradually the war ended. By the time camp was over, the two groups actually asked to go home on the same bus. And when the bus stopped for a rest break, the groups decided to pool their prize money so that everyone could buy malts.

Sherif and his colleagues were entirely aware of the larger implications of their research. In their various reports of the experimental results, they emphasized that nations can coexist peacefully only if they develop meaningful joint goals. On the basis of these studies, Sherif made an impassioned plea:

> The broadening of human bonds is the prerequisite for morality in dealing with peoples outside the narrow in-group bounds, for creation of a widening sense of "we-ness." . . .
>
> The trend is towards larger and larger dependence between peoples and toward the formation of organizations encompassing them. Historical evidence and empirical data of social science support this trend, even though they also show great human wear and tear, suffering, and reverses for intervals of time.
>
> The great question is whether the trend toward interdependence will be permitted to culminate in the standards of conduct required from all, despite stubborn, last-ditch opposition by islands of resistance, or whether the trend will collapse in the world wide holocaust of a thermonuclear showdown. (Sherif, 1966, p. 174)

What other discipline stands ready to conduct research on how to rescue *Homo sapiens* from self-extinction? What other discipline would have the chutzpah to draw conclusions about war and peace from research at a summer camp for boys? It may be presumptuous, but it is also fortunate that some science is trying. Indeed, most psychologists would agree that Sherif's study remains one of our most important sources of scientific knowledge about the causes and cures of group hatred.

Social Psychology Challenges Hollywood

In the 1970s, when debate was raging over the impact of violence depicted on television and in the movies, social psychologists put the issue to an experimental test. This time the chutzpah was international: Jacques-Philippe Leyens at the University of Louvain in Belgium designed the study, along with two associates from the United States and one from Brazil.

Leyens, Camino, Parke, and Berkowitz (1975) disconnected the televisions in four dormitories in a private high school for delinquent or homeless boys (yes, again boys!). This alone should have led to violence. But as a substitute, the experimenters provided a special "movie week." Each dormitory saw five films, one each night. In two of the dormitories the boys saw highly violent films, such as *The Dirty Dozen* and *Bonnie and Clyde.* The boys in the other two dormitories saw films without any violence, such as *Lily* and *Daddy's Fiancée.*

During this and the following week, the boys' behavior was observed. Everyone but Hollywood moguls and network programmers can guess the results: Those who saw the violent movies were substantially more violent. While the issue is a complex one, on which a great deal of subsequent research has been done, the Belgium study was a landmark for understanding this topic.

And Hollywood has not been the only target. David Phillips (1983, 1986) has found that both television and newspaper coverage of violence is associated with increases in violence among the general public. For example, in the case of suicide, increased media coverage of particular suicides is associated with increases in not only suicides but also fatal automobile accidents and private-airplane crashes (presuming some of these occurrences are consciously or unconsciously suicidal). When teenage suicides have been the topic, the more widespread the coverage, the more widespread has been the incidence of suicide.

Even more surprising is Phillip's finding of a 12.46 percent increase in homicides on the third and fourth days following heavyweight championship prizefights between 1973 and 1978. The greatest increases occurred after the most publicized fights, and there was a clear tendency for the victims of homicides on these days to be of the same race as the loser of the fight! Further, the homicides did not decrease after the rise following a fight, as they would have had the boxing matches merely precipitated inevitable homicides rather than causing additional homicides. Nor was gambling a factor, as homicides have not been shown to increase after a Superbowl game.

And what about watching sexual violence? Edward Donnerstein and Leonard Berkowitz (1981) at the University of Wisconsin set up a complicated experiment to examine this issue. In their study, male students were first angered by a person who they believed was another subject (but who in fact was a confederate of the experimenter). Then they watched a film. And then finally they gave what they thought were electric shocks to the supposed "other subject," on the pretense that the shocks were part of a completely separate "learning" experiment that included giving shocks as punishment for mistakes. (You will see later—especially in chapter 5—that such complicated and seemingly artificial experimental procedures can be extremely real to the participant and thus can sometimes yield very provocative results.)

After seeing an aggressive-erotic film in which a woman was a victim, the male student subjects gave more intense shocks when the person supposedly receiving the shocks was female. In contrast, subjects who saw a film that was just as erotic but involved no violence gave no more shock, to either a male or a female recipient, than after watching a nonerotic, nonaggressive film (a tape of a talk-show interview).

Of course, one cannot be sure that people in general will behave like Wisconsin undergraduates or that giving more intense shocks in a laboratory is similar to committing assault in a dark parking lot. Still, while politicians and the media simply speculate about such issues as what kinds of films the video-rental stores ought to be discouraged from carrying, social psychologists are applying scientific methods to these questions.

Social Psychology Challenges the Alleged Apathy of the Whole Human Race

In New York City during the spring of 1964, Kitty Genovese was brutally murdered while thirty-eight people watched from the safety of their apartment windows. The public was appalled. Why didn't anyone try to help? How could people be so callous?

At this time, Bibb Latane and John Darley were two young social psychologists in New York City—Latane at Columbia University and Darley at NYU—and in their separate social circles each was constantly being asked to explain the outrageous circumstances surrounding the Genovese murder. Finally one night Latane and Darley were invited to the same party and, upon meeting, began to commiserate about the nuisance it was to be a social psychologist with no explanation for the failure of bystanders to stop that woman's murder. After the party, Latane and Darley went out to dinner and then to Latane's apartment in Greenwich Village, continuing to talk about the case. What made it so upsetting? Wasn't part of the uproar the *number* of people who had done nothing—not two or three but thirty-eight?

Which led them to wonder whether the large crowd wasn't part of the cause. How did the police know that exactly thirty-eight had watched? Some of the witnesses must have been sufficiently aware of one another to count. Could the number of others watching have actually inhibited people from helping?

And thus a research plan was born. Student volunteers were told they were participating in a study in which they would discuss with one or more other volunteers the problems of living in a big city. This discussion would occur over an intercom, because each discussant was (supposedly) in a separate room. Only one person could speak at a time, in a systematic rotation of turns. Further, the students were told that no one outside of the experiment's participants would hear any of the discussion and that their identities would remain anonymous.

In actuality, only one student was present for each experimental session. A tape recording was the other "participant" (or "participants"—in other conditions, there were up to four other tape recordings). The first tape-recorded "participant" began describing his problems living in New York, including a special problem of experiencing occasional seizures. Next, the true subject gave a two-minute talk. Then, in those conditions in which others were supposed to be present, the others talked, yet again, the only true participant, the subject, was actually hearing tape recordings.

The subject was then told that there would be a second round of discussion, beginning again with the "participant" who had mentioned the seizures. This time, after the taped voice had spoken normally for a while, he began to stammer: "I er um I think I I need er if if could er er somebody . . . help me out it would . . . er s-s-sure be good . . . uh I've got a a one of the er sei er . . ." and so forth, including choking sounds and ending with "I'm gonna die er . . . help er er seizure er [chokes, then quiet]" (Latane & Darley, 1970, pp. 95–96).

Latane and Darley found that if the students thought they were the only ones listening, 85 percent jumped up and went to the next room to help before the victim had finished. But if they thought there were four other students listening, only 31 percent did so. Thus Latane and Darley discovered a peculiar paradox: The more people who witness a person in need, the less likely any one of them will be to help.

Social Psychology Sets Out to Resolve the Great Issues of Philosophy

Of course, social psychologists do not limit themselves to mundane, practical topics like war and peace. They tackle, with equal aplomb, those Great Issues which have stymied the most brilliant philosophers, essayists, and poets throughout the ages. Love, happiness, life, death—social psychology has hauled them all out for experimental analysis.

Love did not become a topic until the late 1960s, not because social psychologists thought it too hard to study but because many considered it too trivial. A few graduate students felt otherwise, and in the late 1960s they devised some ingenious experiments.

At the University of Michigan, Zick Rubin completed a doctoral dissertation in which he found that couples who spent more time gazing into each other's eyes did indeed score higher on a paper-and-pencil questionnaire that Rubin called the "love scale." His 1970 article entitled "The Measurement of Romantic Love" describes this scale.

At about the same time, one of us (A. Aron, 1970), provoked all kinds of havoc as a doctoral student at the University of Toronto by studying love and power. Fortunately, his enthusiastic thesis adviser, John Arrowood, was—you guessed it—a former student of Schachter and of other students of Kurt Lewin.

In this study, male student volunteers participated in a series of tasks with an attractive female student they believed to be another experimental subject. Actually, however, she was in league with the experimenter, and the tasks were rigged so that in both physical and verbal conflicts, she acted (a) strong, (b) weak, or (c) strong and then yielding. As predicted, the subjects were more attracted to the woman in those conditions in which she acted strong then yielding. (See chapter 5.)

One of the first and most influential studies of love was conducted in the mid-sixties by Elaine Walster and her colleagues (1966) at the University of Wisconsin. (She is now Elaine Hatfield and at the University of Hawaii.) The goal was to test experimentally whether people are attracted to the best-looking members of the opposite sex or to someone about as attractive as themselves.

While the poets and novelists offered their own answers and U.S. senators publicly stated that love should not be studied scientifically (or researched with taxpayers' money), Hatfield and her associates went ahead and invited students to a dance for which their dates were to be selected by computer. As the students registered, they were surreptitiously rated for their physical attractiveness by four other students. Then they were "matched" with a date for the dance. Actually, unknown to them, the match was entirely random. During the intermission the students completed questionnaires about how attracted they were to their date. Six months later, all the participants were recontacted to see if they had tried to go out again with their "match" for the dance. The findings were unexpected and clear: Whether handsome or homely themselves, the students were more likely to try to go out again with the better-looking dates.[5]

The impact of those first experiments on love is also clear now: In the seventies and eighties, the study of love and of the close relationships that love develops has exploded into a major subspecialty of social psychology (see chapter 3).

If the mysteries of love can be penetrated, why not the vagaries of happiness? Social psychologist Philip Brickman at Northwestern University, along with Dan Coates and Ronnie Janoff-Bulman (1978), took on the eminently philosophical question of whether happiness is relative. In the long run, how does good fortune or tragedy really affect happiness?

They questioned twenty-two persons who had recently won major prizes in the Illinois State Lottery, twenty-nine who had recently suffered a serious accident and become paraplegic, and twenty-two ordinary individuals. After an average of six months from the event, the people in all three groups reported themselves to be about equally happy. All averaged above the midpoint on a six-point scale ranging from "not at all" to "very much." And their expectations about their future happiness showed no difference at all.

And if love and happiness can be studied, why not the meaning of life itself?

Through the centuries, philosophers have speculated that life lasts so long as it has meaning, purpose, and free will. Ellen Langer and Judith Rodin (1976; Rodin & Langer, 1977) decided

---

[5]While subsequent studies have found nearly the same results for pairs who were first meeting, pairs in already-intact couples have been found to have *similar* levels of attractiveness. For example, Jack McKillip and Sharon Riedel (1983) had teams of student interviewers approach a total of 336 couples, whom they located in shopping centers, the student union, bars, and even in a line waiting to see a play. While one student interviewed each couple about how they saw their relationship, two others rated the attractiveness of each member. McKillip and Riedel found little similarity of appearance among those who saw their relationship as "casual" but did find considerably more similarity than one would expect by chance among those who saw their relationship as "committed." The reasons for the apparent contradiction between studies of what people seem to prefer and what they end up with are still in hot dispute (e.g., Kalick & Hamilton, 1986; Aron, 1988).

to test this idea experimentally by increasing the meaning in the lives of certain aged residents of a Connecticut nursing home. Residents on one floor of the home attended a meeting in which the nursing-home administrator gave a talk emphasizing the control they had over their lives:

> I was surprised to learn that many of you don't . . . realize the influence you have over your own lives here. Take a minute to think of the decisions you can and should be making. For example. . . . This brings me to another point. If you are unsatisfied with anything here, you have the influence to change it. . . . Also, I want to give you each a present. . . . [A box of small plants was passed around, and the patients were given two decisions to make: first, whether or not they wanted a plant at all, and second, to choose which one they wanted.] The plants are yours to keep and take care of as you'd like. . . . One last thing . . . we're showing a movie two nights next week. . . . You should decide which night you'd like to go, if you choose to see it at all. (Langer & Rodin, 1976, pp. 193–94)

Three days later, the director visited each patient and repeated parts of the message.

A comparable group of residents on another floor of the same nursing home were treated to a similar meeting and visits, except that for them the message stressed the staff's responsibility for the patients. There was no emphasis on the residents' responsibility, they were given a plant but no choice as to which one, they were told the nurses would take care of the plants for them, and they were assigned a movie night.

Three weeks later, the residents who had been encouraged to take responsibility for their own lives were happier, more active, and more alert. A year and a half later, these same residents who had received the responsibility message were rated as more vigorous and social by nurses and in better health by doctors. Above all, 85 percent were still alive, whereas among residents on the other floor, only 70 percent were still alive.

Kurt Lewin would have loved this study. It is daring. It has social significance. And it shows a lot of chutzpah.

In Conclusion: Where Chutzpah Comes From and Where It Goes

Now that we have sampled the broad range of audacious topics social psychologists have taken on, perhaps we can see this chutzpah in a clearer light. To a certain extent it comes from the nature of the field—the study of the interaction between individuals and social forces. In this arena significant conflicts occur; intense influences push and shove; outcomes dramatically affect everyday life. It would almost be hard to plan a social psychology study that would *not* be a potential conversation piece.

Still, other fields of psychology are potentially as relevant and riveting, yet they generally lack this bold approach. That seems to be simply because chutzpah has not been part of their historical development, whereas in social psychology a generous display of chutzpah has been a social norm from the beginning. Idealistic graduate students with unusual ideas to test were sought and encouraged by their departments. Bold studies of real-life situations were more likely to be accepted for publication by the editors of social psychology journals. And within certain limits, the more difficult and controversial a topic, the more admiration its researchers received when they made scientific sense out of it.

Most of the social psychologists we spoke with were proud of this aspect of their field. For example, when we asked Bob Zajonc about chutzpah, he explained:

> I think that I would call that aspect taking risks. You don't do interesting research if you don't take risks. Period. If you just prove the obvious, that's not interesting research. The risks may come because the problem is socially delicate, or the risks may come because the problem is intellectually difficult. But usually problems that involve some risks are problems that involve some payoff.

Every discipline has its own history, culture, and social norms. They decide what is worth studying, what methods are appropriate, and what assumptions can be made. These attitudes are passed on from teacher to student and maintained also by journal editors and the hiring practices of academic departments. One can (and probably should, to a certain extent) think of these as limits or blinders placed on the researchers by their field's culture. But as in any culture, these limits also have value: They save the time of those who come after. They don't "reinvent the wheel" or "go down blind alleys." Instead, those who follow are encouraged to build on those who came before. Finally, if it happens that one of a science's norms is *not* to be conservative but to attack new problems with new methods, then its culture is encouraging its own continual regeneration by more or less protecting its own members from itself. Now that's real chutzpah!

2

"Lemmings Overrule Dissidents and Choose Seashore Conference Site"

Social Psychology Emphasizes Social Influence

IMAGINE you are a skin cell (we know it sounds ridiculous, but do it). Your job is to toss out bundles of chemicals when told to, to shrivel up tight when told to, to stand your ground when bumped, and generally to keep up your borders. Food and water gets delivered when you need it. Now and then a nice thrill runs through you and your neighbors. When you're in the mood, you reproduce yourself. It's a good life.

Given your well-regulated behavior, if you thought about yourself at all you would be unlikely to think of yourself as an independent cell, doing your own thing, free to leave when you felt like it, free to reproduce yourself ad infinitum. You would know that you were part of a body. If you left, you would die. If you quit and the others around you quit, the body would die. If you quit and the others did not quit, you would get shoved aside, you would shrivel up, and . . . But you couldn't quit, anyway. Your place is Left Forearm, Human Being. You know no other life.

Human beings are equally enmeshed in their families, jobs, and society—yet frequently see themselves as independent. In a way, social psychology is something of a crusade: The goal is to make the people of the world realize they are part of a social organism, as much as a cell is part of a body. To social psychologists, it is as though humans are under some spell that keeps them from seeing the social context of their lives. And as psychologists, they want to break that spell.

Why? Some just want you to see the truth. Some hope that when things go wrong, you will know to blame yourself or others a little less sometimes and to blame the wider social situation a little more. Others hope that once you are aware of social influences you will be able to resist them when it would be better to do so. Still others hope you will spontaneously do more for the health of the social organism if you see your dependence on it.

But whatever the reason, most social psychologists strive to make people see that social influences determine their thoughts, attitudes, perceptions, emotions, and even their very selves. Modern social psychology arose in part from the thinking of Charles Horton Cooley, who expressed it vividly when he said we possess only a "looking glass self" (1902). Other significant early social psychologists, such as George Herbert Mead and his followers, built their entire theory of social psychology mainly on this theme. The very definition of social psychology is that it studies how people "are influenced by the actual, imagined, or implied presence of others" (Allport, 1968, p. 3).[1]

In every decade, social psychologists have tried to make their point in some new, dramatic, emphatic way. Lewin said it was *outdated* to think of people's behavior as caused only by their

[1]Although Allport's definition of the field focuses on social influence, among social psychologists he was unusually partial to the role of personality in social behavior. For example, Tom Pettigrew, who was later winner of both the distinguished Lewin Memorial Award and the Allport Intergroup Relations Research Prize, was a student of Gordon Allport's at Harvard. Pettigrew recalls proudly showing his adviser his first publication—a study showing the relationship between desegregation and various economic and other social statistics. The six-foot-four Allport looked up from his desk and said, "This is all very interesting, but tell me about the wise judge, the brave mayor." The important cause for Allport was the person, not the social situation.

inner characteristics. He called that the "Aristotelian approach" because it was concerned with "essences." The new, social psychology approach, he insisted, is to see behavior as an interaction of a person's past social experiences and his or her current social situation. This he called the "Galilean approach," the basis of modern science, which is concerned with "forces."

In the 1960s a personality and social psychologist, Walter Mischel, set psychology on its ear by saying that a knowledge of the inner personalities of people allows even a well-trained psychologist to predict almost *nothing* about what those people will do in the next moment, whereas knowing concrete facts about their immediate social situation allows anyone to predict a great deal about their behavior. (If you think about it, the fact that you are reading this book right now gives much more information about your behavior—you are sitting still and looking at the page—than any personality test score could possibly tell.)

Virtually all the nearly fifty social psychologists we interviewed in the process of writing this book said their main message to students and to the world was, in Russ Fazio's words, "the incredible power of the social." And no doubt we will hear new, more dramatic statements of that point in the future.

It takes a lot of chutzpah to embark on such a campaign. In Western cultures especially, people seem to like to think of themselves as rugged individuals who control their own destiny, succeed or fail according to their own efforts, and base their beliefs and feelings, and certainly their perceptions, on direct, rational, "objective" experience. Is this a good cause for a crusade? Or something more like tilting at windmills? Do you think you really aren't *quite* as tightly enmeshed in society as a cell is embedded in a body?

All right, then cut yourself free and imagine for a few minutes that you are the only person in the world. (Yet you have somehow managed to survive and reach adulthood. Don't ask us how!) Your first thought is probably that you would lack the comforts provided by technology. That is a good point. Science, technology, agricultural techniques—society has developed them all and passed the knowledge on from generation to generation. But that would be the least of your problems. Your very ability to think about the situation would be extremely limited. How would you think without language?

Worse, you would probably be listless and lonely, whether you knew why or not (animals raised in total isolation are not very happy looking beasts either). Any meaning to life beyond survival—love, success, having your efforts appreciated, power, even laughter—almost all the pleasures of life are tightly bound up with other people.

You also would know very little. What is poisonous to eat, when and where it is safe to sleep, the function of your brain, your stomach, your lungs—all these things would have to be learned from scratch, for in fact you only know them because someone else has told you. This authority in turn relied on still others: the few people who actually found out for themselves. If so much of what we accept to be "objectively" true is really social knowledge, think how much more social are your political and moral "realities," such as the importance of democracy or the sacredness of human life.

Now we hope you have gotten the message. But how would you get it across to others? As Ellen Berscheid, an eminent researcher and a recent president of the Society for Personality and Social Psychology, said, "Social influence is one of the great, great influences in nature . . . tremendously powerful . . . yet you can't see it."

Of course, as Berscheid added, you can't see electricity or gravity either. But through ingenious experiments, physicists proved the existence of these basic forces. Similarly, social psychologists are demonstrating the existence of this other basic, powerful, invisible force. The purpose of this chapter is to examine some of the ways they are accomplishing this feat, by looking at studies in four areas: how social factors determine how we think, see, feel, and know ourselves. We'll begin with a simple enough study, a pioneering effort by Theodore Newcomb, done in 1934 at Bennington College in Vermont, just after the college's founding.

Other People Influence What We Think

The story of how Ted Newcomb became a social psychologist is as clear a case of social influence as his research. Newcomb's father was a minister and Ted Newcomb intended to become a minister too—except that the seminary he attended was across the street from Columbia University. This was the 1920s and Gardner Murphy was there, talking enthusiastically about this new field of social psychology. (Muzafer Sherif would arrive at Columbia in 1931.) Many of America's other great early psychologists were also at Columbia—for example, Edward Thorndike and Robert S. Woodworth.

The seminary across the street was being attended not only by Newcomb, but by Carl Rogers, Rensis Likert (who later helped invent the opinion survey), Ernest Hilgard (who was to author a leading text and become an authority on self-theory and hypnosis), and Lois Barclay (who later became Lois Barclay Murphy, who collaborated with Gardner Murphy on their pioneering social psychology text, as well as making many substantial independent contributions, primarily in the social psychology of child development). Fascinated by psychology, these seminarians began to spend more and more time over at Columbia. The more they associated with one another and with Columbia's graduate students in psychology, the less they felt like future theologians and the more they felt like future social scientists. In Newcomb's case, a certain class in "New Testament Exegesis" was the last straw: When the professor gave an entire lecture on the meaning of a single Greek word, which he promised to continue explaining during the next class meeting, Newcomb changed schools.

It is not surprising that Ted Newcomb came "to see individual psychological processes within a matrix of group influences" (1974, p. 374).

In 1934 Newcomb took a job teaching at a recently established "experimental" college for women. Bennington College was very exclusive and most of the students were from wealthy, politically conservative families. The faculty, however, were largely liberal, many even radical. Thanks to the events of the Great Depression and his own education, even Newcomb, the minister's son, voted for Socialist Norman Thomas in the 1932 presidential election and was deeply concerned about the Spanish civil war. Thus the women at Bennington were moving from one context—a conservative family and social life—into a new context, wherein the respected figures, the faculty, held diametrically opposed views.

Newcomb immediately saw his chance to demonstrate in a natural setting his belief that "membership in established groups usually involves the taking on of whole patterns of interrelated . . . attitudes" (1958, p. 265). He spent his first year at Bennington preparing his attitude tests. Then in 1935 he launched his version of the social-influence crusade by testing the political attitudes of the arriving freshman class. After that, all he had to do was to sit back and let the liberal attitudes of the college do its work and to measure the attitudes of this group of students every year until they graduated.

What he found was quite straightforward. With each semester at Bennington, students became increasingly liberal in their politics. By the time they were seniors, and often much sooner, they had totally reversed their political course.

Some were well aware of the process, but it made no difference. Explained one senior, "I simply got filled with new ideas here, and the only possible formulation of all of them was to adopt a radical approach" (p. 273). Another said, "I'm easily influenced by people whom I respect, and the people who rescued me when I was down and out, intellectually, gave me a radical intellectual approach" (p. 273). Yet another said, "I was so anxious to be accepted that I accepted the political complexion of the community here" (p. 273).

Those few students who did not change their attitudes were the ones who spent their vacations with their parents, wrote home a lot, and generally maintained their parents' society as their own culture. Newcomb, thanks to some conversations much later with Muzafir Sherif, eventually came to term the group with which one holds common attitudes one's *reference group.*

Other People Influence What We See

Okay, political attitudes are amorphous. We change them all the time. But how about what we see? Will a 5-inch line look 3 inches long just because our reference group says it is so? According to a study by Solomon Asch, you'd better believe it.

Asch was another Columbia student, sometime after Newcomb and before Sherif. He started out more interested in the psychology of learning than in social psychology. But he was studying with some of the founders of the Gestalt school of psychology, which emphasizes the role of patterns, context, and holistic qualities in perception. Gestalt psychology has always been closely connected to social psychology because of Lewin's insistence that what we see is determined by the *whole* context, including social influences; Lewin was himself considered a part of the Gestalt school. And when Asch did research on how people perceive one another, it was very *social* research. (We'll discuss this work in chapter 4.) His most famous study, the "Asch conformity study," is what we will describe here, after we tell you about the boyhood experience that led to it.

Solomon Asch was Jewish, and as a boy he had attended more than one Passover seder. If you have ever been to a seder, you know that traditionally a place is set for Elijah the prophet, including a cup of wine. At a certain point in the ceremony the door is opened. Asch recounted to us what happened at this point at one such seder when he was young:

> I asked my uncle, who was sitting next to me, why the door was being opened. He replied, "The prophet Elijah visits this evening every Jewish home and takes a sip of wine from the cup reserved for him."
>
> I was amazed at this news and repeated, "Does he really come? Does he really take a sip?"
>
> My uncle said, "If you watch very closely, when the door is opened you will see—you watch the cup—you will see that the wine will go down a little."
>
> And that's what happened. My eyes were riveted upon the cup of wine. I was determined to see whether there would be a change. And to me it seemed—it was tantalizing, and of course, it was hard to be absolutely sure—that indeed something was happening at the rim of the cup, and the wine did go down a little.

Later, as a researcher, Asch (1958) set up much the same situation, but with scientific controls. He seated male students, one at a time, at a table along with seven other male students for what the student thought was a simple experiment in "visual judgment." The task was to determine which among three comparison lines shown on a large card was equal to a standard line shown on a similar card. Each student around the table said, in turn, which of the three comparison lines he thought matched the standard line. Then two more cards were shown, one with three lines, the other with the line to be matched. A total of eighteen pairs of cards were shown.

The actual perceptual task was simple, and ordinarily virtually everyone would have instantly agreed on what they saw. Thus, it always came as a considerable surprise to the student subject when on the third pair of cards all six of the students who had answered before him unhesitatingly selected a line clearly longer than the comparison line!

The student subject was put in this predicament because, unknown to him, all seven of the other students were not really subjects in the experiment but in league with Asch. They had agreed to answer in prearranged ways on each turn. So on the next card everyone selected a line that was 20 percent too short (4 inches versus 5 inches). On the next card the students all gave the correct answer. But on the next several cards they mostly gave wrong ones. And when they gave "objectively" wrong ones, they always all agreed on which wrong answer they gave and gave their answers without any hesitation.

Few of the true subjects had any idea that the situation had been rigged. When their turn came around on the rigged trials, three-quarters gave, at least once, the same answer as the majority—the "objectively wrong" answer. A third did so more than half the time.

Yielding was not easy, though. Asch reports that many were "nervous," "confused," "doubt-ridden," and "disoriented." But they went along.

Things were no more comfortable for those who did not go along with the majority. They were often quite ill at ease about disagreeing, saying such things as, "Can't help it" and "I always disagree—darn it." In discussing it with the others immediately after the last card, one of them said, "You're *probably* right, but you *may* be wrong." Then, after the true experiment was explained, this subject said he felt "exulted and relieved." He'd often had the feeling of "to heck with it, I'll go along with the rest" (p. 396). Disagreeing with the majority had been a true ordeal.

Of those who did go along with the rest, what were their reasons? Most explanations boiled down to these three: (a) The largest number said that although they did not see the lines the same as the majority, they assumed the majority was correct and their own perceptions must somehow be wrong; (b) a small number said that although they felt they were completely correct, they did not want to say so because they didn't want to look different to the others; and (c) a few said they actually came to see the line lengths as did the majority.

Social psychologists loved this study. It demonstrated so well what they had been saying about social influence. And when people insisted, "I wouldn't go along with something just because other people said it," social psychologists could reply that Asch had gotten these results with normal, intelligent college students. The findings were also substantiated with many other types of people in later experiments.

Nor is being forewarned a sure guarantee. A group of our own students repeated the Asch study with students at Berkeley. They got the usual results, even when subjects said afterward, in response to the explanation of the study, "Oh yes, I remember reading about that in psychology!"

One factor does make a difference, by causing people to conform even more, and that is the ambiguity of the issue. People will give in more easily about opinions and beliefs than about their direct perceptions. Using a procedure developed by Richard Crutchfield (1955) at the University of California, in which participants were each in a separate booth and saw what they thought were other subjects' answers by way of lights on a control panel, two other Berkeley psychologists (Tuddenham & Macbride, 1959), found that subjects even yielded to agreeing that most Americans eat six meals per day! In a study of military officers (reported in Krech, Crutchfield, & Ballachey, 1962), 37 percent agreed that "I doubt whether I would make a good leader" (although none had agreed to that when asked privately in advance). Most dramatic for the serious point that the social psychologists wanted to make is that 58 percent of college students were pressured by this procedure into agreeing to the proposition that "Free speech being a privilege rather than a right, it is proper for a society to suspend free speech whenever it feels itself threatened" (p. 509). That would be a majority if it had come to a vote. (Only 19 percent had agreed to the statement when questioned privately in advance.)

Obviously, conformity experiments require some heavy-handed deception of the participants. When Stanley Milgram, who had worked extensively with Asch, created the ultimate version of these studies, he finally raised the ethical furor that many felt should have come long before.

It was clear that those excited by the Asch and Crutchfield studies had had Nazi Germany in mind—how had all those people agreed to Hitler's horrible plans?[2] The need for an answer to this question was how Milgram rationalized the ordeal he put his subjects through, a demonstration not only of conformity but of outright obedience to authority, no matter what. Now for the humbling details.

Forty men between twenty and fifty years old were recruited to participate in a study of "memory and learning" at prestigious Yale University via ads in New Haven–area newspapers (Milgram, 1963). When a participant arrived, he and what he believed was another subject (actually an accomplice of the experimenter) would draw papers from a hat for the roles of "teacher" or "learner" in an experiment on the role of punishment in learning. It was rigged so that the true subject always became the "teacher"—both papers in the hat said "teacher."

---

[2]Dorwin Cartwright (1979) went so far as to say that the single person who had the most impact on social psychology was Adolf Hitler. It is easy to see why. Hitler lived at the time when social psychology took shape and drove many of its leading scholars, who had been scattered around Europe, to the East Coast of the United States. There they huddled together, angry and confused, and went to work on the task of getting even, or at least getting clearer about what had happened in Germany. Hitler raised questions about humanity's weakness in the face of social pressure that society wanted answered and was willing to support social psychologists to study. He was also the cause of a war effort in the United States that brought leading psychologists together to work for the first time, with ample funds, on practical social problems.

The two were then taken into the next room, where the true subject watched as the "learner" was firmly strapped, "to prevent excessive motion," into an "electric chair." Electrode paste was applied "to avoid blisters and burns," and electrodes were attached to the "learner's" wrist. The "learner" had four buttons to press to indicate his response to the learning questions he would be asked.

The "teacher" was then taken to an adjoining room, where he was seated at a very professional looking "shock generator," which had switches on it for generating shocks that went in 15-volt increments from 15 to 450 volts. Each set of three switches had a label above it, ranging from "Slight Shock" through "Strong Shock" and all the way up to "Danger: Severe Shock." Finally, over the very last two switches, of 435 and 450 volts, the label just said "XXX." To demonstrate the apparatus and further convince the subject of the reality of the situation, the subject, or "teacher," was given as a sample a real shock of 45 volts, using the third switch on the generator.

As you might have guessed, the whole thing was a ruse and the shock generator was not even connected to the electrodes that were fastened to the learner. The sample shock came from a 45-volt battery inside the shock generator. But in virtually every case the subject was quite convinced by the whole thing.

Next, each subject was shown how to teach the "learner" a list of word pairs. One pair was to be given at a time, and the "learner" had to indicate the correct match from four alternatives by pressing one of the buttons. The "learner's" choice showed up on a panel on the shock generator. Whenever he made a wrong guess, the "teacher" was supposed to shock him, increasing the shock by 15 volts (one switch) with each wrong guess.

Then the experiment began. The "learner" made some right and some wrong guesses but missed enough so that the stakes kept getting higher. The "teachers" sweated and laughed nervously but kept giving the shocks. If a "teacher" complained, the experimenter instructed him to continue.

The subjects had been told in advance that their small payment was theirs just for showing up. They could keep it no matter what. There was nothing preventing the "teacher" from just getting up and leaving. Yet *every single one of them* continued up to 300 volts, one of the switches marked "Intense Shock."

At this point, the "learner" pounded loudly on the wall—all part of the ruse—and did not give any answer to the test question. The experimenter told the "teacher" to treat no answer as a wrong answer and to continue. Finally, at this stage, five subjects walked out.

Then at 315 volts, the first switch under "Extreme Intensity Shock," the "learner" again pounded on the wall and again gave no answer. Four more subjects left. But the rest continued. The "learner" was not heard from again.

The "teachers" administering the "shocks" were not taking their job lightly. They would "sweat, tremble, stutter, bite their lips, groan, and dig their fingernails into their flesh" (p. 375). More than a third of them laughed nervously or smiled, saying later it was definitely not because they were enjoying themselves. Three of the "teachers" had "full blown uncontrollable seizures" (p. 375). A forty-six-year-old encyclopedia salesman had a seizure so severe that the experiment had to be stopped. But the others, twenty-six of the original forty subjects—postal clerks, high school teachers, engineers, salesmen, and the like—continued to the maximum, "XXX" shock of 450 volts.

After the experiment ended, to each subject's considerable relief, and after everything was explained to them, Milgram reported that he took care to ensure that the subjects "would leave the experiment in a state of well being" (p. 374). But finally the deceptions required in conformity experiments were brought into question. Because the subjects had been so upset by the experience during the proceedings, Milgram was strongly criticized by many psychologists (for example, Baumrind, 1964) for not stopping this research when he saw the effect it was having. And while other social psychologists believe some of the intensity of this criticism was due to the unpleasantness of the findings, all have taken to heart the ethical questions raised by Milgram's study. Today very few social psychologists would conduct such an experiment, and very few universities would permit them to do so if they tried. (Milgram [1964], however, felt quite justified. The subjects told him they had learned from the experience. A long-term follow-up and examination of subjects by "an independent medical examiner," a psychiatrist, seemed to confirm this conclusion.)

Whatever the rightness or wrongness of Milgram's experiment, it reveals something fundamental about obedience and clearly demonstrates the incredible power of social influence. So, too, does the work of yet another social psychologist, Irving Janis of Yale University, who has looked at the practical consequences of social pressure by systematically analyzing the decision-making processes that led to various major mistakes by U.S. presidents and their advisers (for example, the Bay of Pigs invasion, the Watergate cover-up). What he observed in each case was that decisions were made in a group atmosphere that discouraged dissent, a situation he has labeled "groupthink" (Janis, 1972). Everyone wanted to be in harmony with the president and with one another, and their discussions were secret and isolated. Thus the discussants and "advisers" found it difficult to offer an objection based on what they might privately have felt was the wisest course; they found it hard even to evaluate whether they had any independent ideas on the subject.

Other People Influence What We Feel

Stanley Schachter (about whom you learned a little in chapter 1) started one of the most famous sets of studies of social influence by trying to study affiliation (Schachter, 1959). It was already known that people kept in isolation feel anxious, and so Schachter wondered if anxious people would prefer to be with one another. And if so, why?

In his first study, female undergraduates arriving at the laboratory were met by the experimenter, a "Dr. Gregor Zillstein" (played first by Schachter but later by various graduate students), who informed each subject that he was sorry, but the needs of science required that the experiment would involve some strong electric shocks—but not to worry, "There would be no permanent damage." The room was full of apparatus, and it all seemed very believable.

Then the student was told that while the experiment was being set up, she could wait in another room. Offhandedly, Zillstein explained that she could wait either alone or with another female student who was also waiting to be in the experiment. The subjects' choice of where to wait was the true purpose of the experiment. After the choice was made, the subject was "debriefed" and no doubt much relieved.[3]

Schachter found that under these conditions misery loves company. But the next question was, Why did the subjects choose to wait with others? There were two theories: (1) distraction and (2) the need to be with someone to help figure out what you are feeling. Hence, he did a second experiment. In this version, some of the subjects were given the option of waiting either alone or with another student waiting for the same experiment; others were given the option of waiting alone or with students waiting to see their faculty advisers. Theory 1 predicted more choices to wait with another young woman who was waiting for her adviser (she would offer more distraction), and theory 2 predicted more choices to wait with another young woman waiting for the same experiment (so that they could verbally or nonverbally compare what they were feeling). The results supported theory 2. In fact, not one of the subjects wanted to wait with the student waiting to see her adviser!

From this finding, it occurred to Schachter and Jerry Singer, his student at the time, that people probably often use social information to determine what they feel, particularly when what they ought to feel in a situation is not completely clear from objective information. This general idea had been formalized earlier, in reference to self-evaluations of abilities and attitudes, under the name "social comparison theory" (Festinger, 1954). Schachter and Singer (1962) suggested that since

[3]No one ever received any actual shocks in this experiment. However, at an informal get-together of former University of Minnesota social psychology students a few years ago, a recent graduate told how that old dentist's-chair-turned-"shock-chair" that Schachter had used to help scare his subjects was still kept as a revered memento, twenty-five years later. At that point, the older social psychologists present, who had been Schachter's assistants on that study, looked blankly at one another and finally reported to the disillusioned recent graduates that Schachter had never used such a chair in that study!

those studying emotion had not at that time identified clearly different physiological states for different emotions, perhaps emotions arise as a combination of a generalized physiological state of being "stirred up" (arousal of the sympathetic nervous system, to be precise) along with a mental interpretation of that state. Or, as they put it, "The cognition, in a sense, exerts a steering function" (p. 380).

To test this idea, they set up the following experiment. Male introductory psychology students who had volunteered to participate (and whose medical records had been checked by the university health service to be sure the experiment was safe for them) were told they were taking part in a study of the effects on vision of a new vitamin, "suproxin." One at a time, the subjects were given an injection. For most of the subjects it was actually a shot of adrenalin, a hormone that creates physiological effects like those associated with emotion, including the subjectively noticeable changes of "palpitation, tremor, and sometimes a feeling of flushing and accelerated breathing" (p. 382). About 30 percent of the subjects, as a control condition, were given an injection that contained only saline solution, which has no physiological effect at all.

After receiving their shots of, supposedly, "suproxin," some subjects were told that the fictitious drug created such "side effects" as flushing and trembling hands—all the effects known to be produced by adrenalin. Another group was told to expect side effects that in fact would be unlikely to occur from adrenalin (such as itching and numbness of the feet). Finally, yet another group was told that the "suproxin" was "mild and harmless and would have no side effects" (p. 382). The group that received the saline solution was also given this last speech.

Thus, there were four groups. Of those receiving adrenalin, some expected the actual effects adrenalin produces, some expected effects that adrenalin never produces, and some expected no side effects. Those who received the saline solution also expected no side effects. The idea was that those who had a proper explanation for their arousal would be unaffected by anything that subsequently happened to them, whereas those who had no good explanation for an onset of arousal would look to their circumstances for an explanation and manifest an emotion appropriate to those circumstances.

Schachter had pretested the adrenalin injections on his graduate students (an experience well remembered by his victims). He knew that the effect of the size of injection the researchers were giving would be clearly noticed by most subjects about three to five minutes after the injection. Thus, for the subjects to associate the onset of the physiological symptoms with the circumstances, the circumstances had to be created quickly. Accordingly, immediately after the injection, the experimenter brought in to the room another "subject," who was introduced as having just received the same injection but was actually a confederate of the experimenter. The two were then asked to wait for twenty minutes while the "vitamin" took effect.

At this point, half the subjects began what was called the "anger condition." They were asked to complete a questionnaire while they waited, a questionnaire especially designed to create annoyance. In addition, the experimenter's confederate did everything he could to act annoyed about it. In fact, before even looking at the questionnaire, the confederate started complaining about the experiment. He also paced himself to complete items at the same rate as the true subject, complaining about each item: "Boy this is a long one," or "Look at question 9—how ridiculous can you get?" or "That's a real insult."

In fact, there was much to complain about. The first questions were innocuous enough, but personal questions soon followed, such as "What is your father's income?" Then came insulting questions, asking the respondents to identify the member of their families for whom it was most true that he or she "does not bathe or wash regularly" or "seems to need psychiatric care." "None" was not a choice; one member of the family had to be listed.

At about this point, the bogus subject ripped up the questionnaire and stamped out of the room. If the actual subject continued with the questionnaire on his own, he faced increasingly insulting items. The last asked, "With how many men (other than your father) has your mother had extramarital relationships?" The lowest multiple-choice answer was "4 and under."

The other half of the subjects participated in what was called the "euphoria condition."[4] In this condition, when the experimenter left the true subject and the bogus subject in the room together, there was no questionnaire to fill out; instead, they were told that while they were waiting they could make use of any rubber bands, paper, or anything else in the room.

Immediately, the experimenter's confederate started doodling. Then he crumpled up his paper and started playing basketball with it and the wastebasket, making comments such as "two points" and "the old jump shot is really on today." If the true subject did not join in spontaneously, he was invited to.

Next, the confederate started making first paper airplanes and then a slingshot; then he located an old Hula-Hoop and played with it. All the while he was the essence of friendliness, inviting the subject to join in the fun.[5]

Throughout the "waiting period," the subjects were being watched through a one-way mirror and the extent of their participation was being recorded. Of course, the procedure was "double blind": Neither the confederate nor the raters were allowed to know what injection and what information the subject had received.

Following their wait and before the expected eye test, the subjects completed some questionnaires on various topics. Buried among them were a couple of questions on their current mood.

---

[4]Actually, approximately four-sevenths were in the euphoria condition. Half of each group that expected some side effect was in each emotion condition, except that all of the group that expected irrelevant side effects were in the euphoria condition.

[5]The confederate in the euphoria condition was Bibb Latane—a tall, lanky, red-haired young student of Schachter's at the time but whom you will remember from chapter 1 as the researcher with John Darley in the bystander-apathy study conducted in the wake of the Kitty Genovese murder. Latane had decided only at the last minute to become a social psychologist rather than a lawyer, and he remembers thinking during the experiment that "It was a far cry from law school to be standing on tabletops spinning Hula-Hoops."

The results were a bit complicated.[6] But the overall finding was quite clear: Those who got adrenalin and had been told to expect the adrenalin effects as "side effects" showed very little emotion. They did not join in much with the confederates, and they did not indicate much mood change in the final questionnaire. Similarly, those who got the saline solution and were not physiologically aroused also showed little emotion, either in their behavior or on the questionnaire. Subjects in these conditions often just sat there while the confederate went through his bizarre antics.

But those who were aroused and either had no explanation for their symptoms or had been given the wrong explanation strongly showed the emotion of the condition they were in. In fact, in the euphoria condition one subject "threw open the window and, laughing, hurled paper basketballs at passersby." Another "jumped on the table and spun one hula hoop on his leg and the other on his neck."

Jerry Singer remembers this as an experiment that not only was fun to do but felt important scientifically:

> The ability to see people being manipulated into one or another emotion simply on the basis of what a model was doing was such a striking demonstration of behavior. And the ability of this nonspecific drug to bring it about just seemed a source of wonder.

Other People Influence What We *Are*

Social psychologist Robert Rosenthal (Rosenthal & Fode, 1963) at Harvard started out studying social influence in an odd way—

[6]Basically, the problem was that some of those who got adrenalin did not become physiologically aroused, some of those who got saline did become aroused, and some of those who got adrenalin and were told to expect no side effects did in fact attribute their arousal to the injection. If, however, on the basis of various measures of these things, one eliminates subjects who fell into these three categories of responses inappropriate to instructions, the results reported here hold up quite nicely. Schachter and Singer also report several other studies that confirm their result. The variation was probably largely due to the injection itself. The researchers did consider some alternatives to the injection procedure that might have obviated the problems (for example, "ventilating the experimental room with vaporized adrenalin"), but these alternatives were not practical.

by randomly assigning rats of the same strain to two groups of students who were to teach the rats to run a maze. One group of students was told that they had bright rats, the other that they had dull ones. The allegedly "bright" rats were consistently better at learning to run mazes, apparently because, according to questionnaires, the students found these rats more "likable" and so handled them quite differently.

Fascinated by these results, Rosenthal and Lenore Jacobson (1968) did the same study in a classroom, telling elementary school teachers that they had certain students in their classes who were "academic spurters." In fact, these students were selected at random; absolutely nothing else was done by the researchers to single out these children. Yet by the end of the school year, 30 percent of the children arbitrarily named as spurters had gained an average of 22 IQ points, and almost all had gained at least 10 IQ points. The "spurters" were also rated much higher in their classroom performance by their teachers. Rosenthal compared his results with those of an expensive, government-funded "total push" campaign that led, after three years, to gains that were much smaller than even the gains for the control students in these classrooms. Something had definitely happened to the teachers of these students.

Rosenthal was fairly certain the teachers did not spend more time with the alleged "spurters," because these students improved less on their verbal scores than on their reasoning scores. Rather, he thought the teachers were more excited about teaching these students and maybe about teaching generally. And they must have subtly communicated respect for and enthusiasm about these students, so that the students themselves felt more capable of understanding and anticipated better performance from themselves. Rosenthal calls this the "Pygmalion effect." Others call it the "Rosenthal effect." And still others see it as a special case of what has come to be called "self-fulfilling prophecy."

Social psychologists love studies that demonstrate how much social influences determine a person's self-image. A favorite such study was conducted by Mark Snyder, Beth Tanke, and Ellen Berscheid (1977) at the University of Minnesota, some years after the "Dr. Zillstein" era. At the time, Snyder was studying the effects of self-fulfilling prophecy and Berscheid was researching interpersonal attraction. Thus it was natural for them, together with their graduate student at that time, Tanke, to design an experiment to look at self-fulfilling prophecy in the area of attractiveness.

It was quite a complicated experiment to carry out (as Tanke put it, "in the grand tradition" of Asch, Schachter, et al.), involving considerable staging and management of when and where subjects would show up. Students were told they were participating in a study on "the processes by which people become acquainted with each other" (p. 659). A male and a female subject would arrive separately and then hold a ten-minute, get-acquainted "phone conversation" through earphones and microphone. The conversation was tape-recorded. The male subject was also given what he thought was a picture of the female subject.

Half the young men were randomly chosen to receive a picture of a young woman, not the experimental partner, who had been independently judged to be attractive, and half received a picture of a young woman who had been independently judged to be unattractive.[7] After the experiment it was no surprise that independent judges, listening to recordings of only the male subject's part of the conversation, could easily pick out which young men were talking to a woman they believed to be "attractive." What was more surprising was that, when listening to only the female subject's half of the conversation, other male college students rated as more attractive those women who had been talking to a male subject who thought he was talking to an attractive woman! In other words, however attractive a

[7]Getting photographs of unattractive young women was not easy. Tanke explained that you cannot simply go up to someone and ask for her picture for the "unattractive condition in an experiment." The researchers first tried a modeling agency, reasoning that the models could make themselves look unattractive with makeup and so forth. The first modeling agency they approached asked if they wanted the models "dressed or undressed." The second modeling agency understood the idea a little better, but the models had such attractive features that all they could do with makeup was to look beat-up and tired, which was not the idea. Finally, the researchers asked some ordinary young women from a neighboring college to "make themselves unattractive" and be photographed for ten dollars. The students had a good time grooming themselves for the part, they did not mind because no one at the University of Minnesota knew them anyway, and the researchers got their needed photos.

woman may have initially thought she was, she becomes much more attractive to men when she is talking with a man who is responding to her as if she is attractive.

Then Are Individual Choices Impossible?

We said at the outset that nearly all social psychologists emphasize the ubiquity of social influence and that one of their major purposes is to help individuals counteract social influence when it pushes them toward doing something immoral, destructive, or limiting to their creativity. Social psychologists want to avoid another Hitler or another McCarthy era; they want to reduce bystander apathy during murders or rapes; they want to help young people resist peer pressure when it pushes them toward life-destroying decisions.

An example is Harry Reis, who emphasizes to his students that they must "stay alert. Think about the way all these things are affecting them without their knowing it. And by becoming more aware of it, asking, 'Hey, do I want it that way?' "

In other words, some social psychologists do believe individuals can make personal choices at least partly free of social influence but only if they are first aware of those influences. Others are perhaps a little less optimistic: They would say that most people cannot resist the influence of their reference group especially but that individuals *can* choose their reference group; they can select which social influences to live under. As Lewin is reputed to have said, "No change in attitude without a change in culture, no change in culture without a change in attitude." And we see this principle dramatized all the time—for example, in the lawyer who first is a political conservative while she is a district attorney and then is a liberal when she becomes a public defender. Normally, we let changes in culture just happen to us, but we can also make choices. If we want to be compassionate, we can associate with unselfish, dedicated types. If we want to be logical, we can hang out with logicians. On a larger scale, we can change society by seeing that institutions like schools, the media, and government provide the "right social influences" for good citizenship. Often these institutions do not recognize, or do not want to recognize, their crucial role.

Or it may be too hard for institutions to change, once again because their members are under social pressure not to deviate. All this makes the social psychologist unpopular sometimes. It is easier, even nicer, to leave the solution of social problems to the individual. Berscheid commented:

> I think many times governments and established institutions do not like the nature of our answers, because very frequently our answers are that your problem is not the people, but the context in which these people are living, working, and operating. You cannot blame them. Their behavior is a product of their nature interacting with this context. A lot of institutions (including universities) don't want to hear this, because they don't want the responsibility to make the kinds of changes that would bring about, for example, improved job performance, reduced violence, or fewer divorces. In not blaming the individual, [social psychologists] take a different approach. But it is a vital one. As a result, I think we are not the darling of the social and behavioral sciences—we are not even the darling of psychology—and I think tomorrow belongs to us.

And Is It All One Way? Can Individuals Never Influence Society?

In spite of their emphasis on society influencing the individual, social psychologists must admit that individuals do influence society, too. They have to admit it because they themselves have often influenced society. Especially if they say that the purpose of their crusade is to show how one can be independent, they thereby imply that independence is possible. Asch, when introducing his group-pressure studies, always explains that he is studying those factors which make people resist group pressure as well as those which make them yield to it. Other social psychologists have also emphasized that with greater knowledge of the process of social influence, individuals can and do have a greater impact, whether they teach students, run for office, rear children, or manage personnel. And perhaps the most significant answer to whether individuals can affect society comes from the lives of social psychologists. By their very work they remind us that every change in society must still come, finally, from the brains of single individuals, thinking in their wonderfully idiosyncratic ways.

But is it enough, especially in a democracy, to be satisfied that at least a few individuals can influence society? A duel among skilled influencers still leaves the less aware people as pawns, a situation that many fear is happening more and more during election campaigns, through clever ads and public relations. On the final page of the most influential social psychology textbook of the early 1960s, the authors (Krech, Crutchfield, & Ballachey, 1962) said that "the crucial problem toward which all the behavioral sciences must be directed is how man can remain an *individual in society*" (p. 529). Which requires the general public becoming thoroughly aware of social forces and how to both resist and use them. Which requires a crusade. And social psychologists have made it theirs.

In Conclusion: Science as Another Social Force

It was once said that humanity received three great blows to its self-esteem: that the earth was not at the center of the universe (Copernicus's doing); that humans evolved from animals (Darwin's blow); and, thanks to Freud, that "rationality" and "civilization" were a cover-up for unconscious, irrational instincts. Social psychologists seem to want to add a fourth: that most of our "individual acts of free will" are guided by situational and social influences.

Many nonscientists, and even many scientists, will tell you that science does not and should not get involved in changing society. Science should only provide information. But of course, as the above examples illustrate, the mere providing of information does affect society—sometimes drastically. Certainly, no one can doubt the impact of nuclear physics on the world.

The fact is that science is giving human beings more influence over everything—the environment, the atom, DNA, and one another—than human society seems ready to use with perfect responsibility. Almost all scientists realize this fact, but most don't like thinking about it much, for it isn't their specialty. Which puts the ball in the court of some of the social sciences and right in front of the racquet of social psychology. Let's hope social psychology can keep up a good volley.

3

"Mirror, Mirror, on the Wall, Who Is the Loveliest Mirror of All?"

Social Psychologists See Social Psychology Everywhere

SOCIAL influence is important not just theoretically to social psychologists; it is a tangible feature of their lives. As social psychologist Phil Shaver explains:

> I feel very aware of . . . [such things as] the kind of power that people yield by virtue of their professional roles, or social-class differences in dress and in confidence in interaction. . . . It's like seeing extra dimensions of what's going on.

Artists see more in a landscape than the rest of us do; physicists see more in the shape of the ocean's waves. The specialty of social psychology is the relationships between people—such issues as how people talk to one another, achieve status and power, become attracted, and reveal their beliefs. Thus it is not surprising that, for example, when we ourselves are sitting at dinner with friends, the lines of attraction or annoyance, the patterns of status and power, the connections of mutual interest—these seem as real as if they were strands strung between people, creating a social net. It's not that we necessarily think about these ties. They are just there. Tangible. Almost visible.

In the Hall of Mirrors

While attending a psychology convention not long ago, one of us was introduced to a fellow social psychologist. We spent several minutes getting acquainted in the usual way for two academics. That is, we played a little duet of simultaneously trying to make an impression on the other while trying to form one: We exchanged information about our status, letting each other know where we'd got our degrees, whom we'd studied with, what we'd published; we measured each other's intellectual sharpness and wit; we searched out each other's potential for providing some new stimulation, perhaps a friendship.

Then, as the conversation was going so well, slowly, very slowly, we revealed something personal about ourselves, and when the other reciprocated, we revealed a little more. All the while we adjusted our postures and the space between us, expressing our growing comfort with the relationship—even while also both feeling rushed by the nature of the setting. After all, the norms are against extended conversations at such conferences, where everyone has many sessions to attend and appointments to keep.

Social psychologists have studied the process of acquaintance in some detail, and the encounter we've just described would not be very different for the meeting of two mathematicians or two plumbers, except for one all-important fact: *We were both completely aware of what was going on.*

Not long ago we asked a few social psychologists about their impressions of the most recent annual cocktail party of the Division of Personality and Social Psychology at the American Psychological Association convention held each August. All of them said something like, "Oh, it was the usual thing . . ." and then proceeded, without a second thought, to give an intricate and sophisticated description of the patterns and processes going on at that party. Never did they comment on the actual content of what was said or who was there. Nothing so mundane as that. Only the social dynamics.

Similarly, Strickland, Aboud, and Gergen (1976) reprinted a transcript of the last session of an international meeting of social psychologists in Canada, at which some graduate students brought up what they saw as the domination of the field by the older, more established members. This topic led to a lively discussion about first the social structure of the field, then the social structure of the current meeting, and next the structure and dynamics of the conversation. Finally, they started discussing why the structure and dynamics of the conversation were the subject of the conversation!

Life for social psychologists is not always a hall of mirrors of social dynamics. Nor are social psychologists always able to use this increased awareness of social realities to any great advantage in their personal lives—they can be wallflowers at a party, just like anyone else. But they can't help but see what is really happening among people. Theodore Sarbin (the iconoclastic applier of role theory to, for example, mental illness and hypnotic trances) put it thusly: "I look at people humanely, but I can't help but see their life stories . . . the social psychological variables."

If you sit two non–chess players before a half-finished game, they see little figures on a checkerboard; set two chess players before that game and they see moves, strategies, triumphs, and follies. It's the same idea.

A Taste for Quasselstrippe

It should be no surprise that people having this ability to see more in social interactions are also fond of involving themselves in social situations. They work in groups, play in groups, study in groups—besides observing themselves in these groups. When interviewing our fellow social psychologists for this book, we often asked how a particular idea was developed. Again and again, we heard, "I don't know how we came up with the idea. We were talking and . . ."

The "we" usually meant a few professors and a few graduate students, working together. When asked about how they gathered to meet—in regular seminars, or lunch meetings, or whatever—the usual response was surprise. Things just worked that way. Everyone was always interacting and thinking as a group.

All the sciences seem to require more of a group effort these days. In fact, life is so complex that almost everything has to be done by teamwork. It is harder and harder to identify the one Great Mind responsible for some idea, be it the computer, the big bang theory, or the design of the clothes you are wearing. Frequently in science, however, the team is composed of an authority surrounded by a bevy of disciples.

In contrast, in social psychology we get the impression that colleagues tend to collaborate more. Even when students do work with a mentor, it is more often on relatively equal footing. This arrangement seems to be as much for the pleasure of having company as it is to generate better ideas and distribute the work load.

Our impression was corroborated by nearly every social psychologist we interviewed. For example, when we asked Marilyn Brewer whether there was anything that distinguishes social psychologists from other psychologists, she said, quite spontaneously, "Yes. They're more social! They tend to form a more cohesive group within a psychology department than other specialties of psychology." Deborah Richardson emphasized that her greatest reward from her work was "the people." And Anthony Pratkanis recalled with nostalgia his days as a graduate student at Ohio State, when every Friday

> we would go out for "team beer." It was real tense at times, but it was just so much fun to have four or five people all thinking the same stuff, just going out and trying to resolve some issue, to think it through, to design an experiment, and say "you were wrong and I was right," or "you were right and I was wrong"—whatever. That was just an absolute thrill for me.

Is this another Lewinian legacy? Certainly Lewin worked this way. Nearly every development of his emerged in a group setting. Lewin's informal group meetings in Berlin, his Quasselstrippe, continued even amid the cornfields of Iowa. His students and colleagues in the American Midwest translated Quasselstrippe as "the Hot-Air Club." Instead of Berlin's Schwedisch Cafe, they met in Iowa City's Round Window Restaurant, where the owner let them use an upstairs room to eat their bag lunches, provided they bought coffee or tea. The lunch meetings were full of "animated conversation, bad puns, and much laughter

. . . with Lewin joining in the fun as much as anyone" (Marrow, 1969, p. 82). In such an atmosphere of group creativity, who could doubt the importance of social influence?

According to several of those we interviewed, the creation of this democratic and intellectually impassioned atmosphere was an explicit goal of many of Lewin's students when they became leading figures in their own right. For example, Leon Festinger (Lewin's most famous student, about whom you will learn more in chapter 6) met regularly with his students at Stanford University over lunch and had them to his house often. And Schachter's students at the University of Minnesota seemed to be constantly meeting in a group, often centered on a game of cribbage. Peals of laughter would emanate from any room they were in. The favorite sport seemed to be "Can you top this idea?" Not a bad pastime for any group of scientists but so much easier in a convivial atmosphere.

Besides enjoying groups, social psychologists are inevitably especially sensitive to social phenomena in groups. They have that ability, they have the training, and they have the love of social life (which came first for any particular social psychologist is hard to say). No wonder social psychologists have conducted enormous amounts of research on their favorite place to be and thing to watch, groups. In fact, the very first social psychology experiment (Tripplett, 1898) was about how much faster people can wind fish line in a group than alone. This chapter is going to give you a taste of that research on groups and of how social psychologists' awareness of group phenomena gave rise to (or sometimes resulted from) many of these studies.

"Herr Quasselstrippe," Kurt Lewin, did, of course, make constant use of groups as both objects of study and methods of study, as well as places to teach and to enjoy himself. One story brings the point home well. Fritz Heider (1983) described attending one of Lewin's seminars at the University of Berlin in the mid-1920s on a day when the subject was embarrassment. Rather than simply talk about it in the abstract, the ebullient Lewin embarrassed some people. He asked a male and a female student to volunteer for a little "experiment." When they agreed, he then asked them to dance in front of the class for several minutes, without music, while the rest of the students sat and watched. (After all, embarrassment, like so many other emotions, occurs only in relation to other people.) Afterward Lewin asked the pair about what they felt and then brought the entire group into the discussion. By the end of class that day, those two students must have had a vivid experience of embarrassment, as seen by watching themselves watch others watch themselves in a musicless waltz in a hall of mirrors.

The Lessons of War

In the United States during World War II, social psychologists, along with almost everyone else, banded together to do their part. Social psychologists applied themselves to everything from surveying soldiers' morale to assessing leadership. For example, as part of the war effort Lewin was asked to find ways to convince housewives to serve the more readily available organ meats, such as liver and brains. He found that those who were led in a group discussion by a Red Cross nutrition expert and encouraged to talk about how to persuade "women like themselves" to help the nation in this way were ten times more likely to serve these meats afterward than those who simply heard a stirring patriotic lecture by the same expert, giving the same factual information.

As a result of all the attention given to existing groups, such as combat units, and the study of groups as a means to accomplish tasks previously done by individuals, the study of groups had, by war's end, a new, practical legitimacy. The war experience had demonstrated that *groups* got work done, that *groups* had morale and moods, and above all, that groups were a powerful tool for changing their members' attitudes and behaviors. Of course, Lewin had not needed convincing, but the significance of groups had been brought home very sharply to all social psychologists. By seeing the war as a huge group effort, applying group principles to it, and then witnessing the unexpected effectiveness of those same groups, social psychologists came to appreciate what a "group effort" really meant.

Immediately after World War II, Lewin established the Research Center for Group Dynamics at the Massachusetts Institute of Technology. This center began a tradition of research

;roups that dominated social psychology through the 1950s continues to play a major role in the field. A typical study his tradition compared the productivity of groups when nized into different communication patterns, looked at how ps treat deviants, or distinguished the different types of :rs that spontaneously emerge during group interaction.

t Lewin was always interested in applying his ideas to real tions. Thus he was frequently asked to try to solve social ems. With the end of the war, one of the most urgently problems was racial and ethnic prejudice. Its effects on Germany and on Europe's Jewish population was still achingly clear, yet black soldiers and veterans belonging to other minorities were returning home to the United States, after having fought as valiantly for their country as any whites, and being treated as second-class citizens. When such discriminatory treatment occurred in public housing, public schools, and public places generally, many government leaders felt it was intolerable. Accordingly, our Superman of Social Psychology again rushed to the rescue, with a plan to organize attitude-changing groups. This time, however, he initiated more than anyone had bargained for. Eventually thousands—perhaps millions—of people took giant steps in their awareness of the intricacies of social life, all thanks in large part to Kurt Lewin. And he certainly taught some social psychologists a thing or two in the process. Let's look at those groups Lewin began.

Getting Sensitive

To many people, the *T-group* (T for training), encounter group, sensitivity training group, or personal growth group was a fad of the 1970s. But before and after its public popularity, it was a serious technique for vividly teaching the patterns and dynamics of social life through direct experience. The T-group was officially born in 1946. We can think of that date as the moment when social psychologists' sensitivity to their own social interactions acquired a formalized technique for its development.

It all began when the Connecticut State Inter-Racial Commission asked Kurt Lewin to teach community leaders some new ways to combat racial and religious prejudice, a favorite topic of Lewin's. He and his cohorts planned a two-week workshop for forty-one selected trainees, mostly educators and social workers, about half of whom were black or Jewish. Lewin simultaneously planned to teach certain social principles, have the trainees experience those principles firsthand, and make all this a research study to identify further the most effective methods of changing people.

In his usual democratic way, Lewin determined that he and all his staff of fellow social psychologists would treat everyone as peers; the group, not the "leaders," would make decisions. Thus, on the very first day, the group worked on making decisions about the next two weeks while some of the researchers sat back to observe the group dynamics. That night the participants had the evening free while the staff met to hear the observers discuss what they had seen. Three of the participants, having nothing planned for the evening, asked Lewin if they could sit in on the staff meeting. Some of the staff predicted mayhem, but Lewin, in his pleasant German accent, probably made his famous response when disagreeing: "Could be, but I sink ozzer."

As one of the staff said about the meeting, it was as if a "tremendous electric charge" went through the room when people first heard their social behavior discussed (Marrow, 1969, p. 212, quoting Bradford). The charge sparked into an open conflagration when one trainee heard an observer's description of her behavior that did not fit with her own experience. She interrupted the staff, and an intense interchange ensued—with Lewin in the middle of it, enjoying himself immensely and turning it into a learning experience for the staff as much as for the trainees.

During this meeting, no one was allowed to wander off into past histories or intellectual rationalizations for his or her behaviors. The topic was the "here and now" of what had happened that day, and clear feedback was the goal. Lewin was cheerfully confident that once people heard how their behavior affected others, they would be able to see for themselves what to change, be motivated to make the change, and be able to give clearer feedback to others. It was the hall-of-mirrors effect again—seeing oneself as others see one, and seeing how one responds to that, and how people react to that response, and how one responds to that reaction, and so forth.

The three trainees gained so much from this feedback about their here-and-now behavior that they asked if they could come back again. By the next night, word had gotten around and all forty-one trainees showed up after dinner to hear the observers talk about how they had behaved and inevitably to discuss those observations.

A few nights later, after one of these meetings, Ronald Lippitt described how some of the staff discussed it "at a hamburger joint" and concluded that these sessions were having a powerful effect on the trainees' ability to bridge the gap between good intentions and actual behavior (Lippitt, quoted in Back, 1972, p. 9). Trainees could receive feedback that made them more sensitive to their behavior, and criticism was brought "into the open in a healthy and constructive way" (Lippitt quoted in Marrow, 1969, p. 212).

All in all, by the end of the two weeks, the evening sessions seemed to have been the most significant part of the workshop. This impression held up during the year after the workshop. The researchers kept track of the participants' efforts to combat discrimination and found they were making excellent progress. When asked about how the workshop had helped them, the trainees reported that their new sensitivity to their own behavior was one of the richest sources of growth, thanks especially to the feedback they had received during those evening sessions.

As a result, the next summer saw the establishment of the National Training Laboratories (NTL) in Bethel, Maine, designed to implement the discoveries of the first workshop by helping train leaders for communities around the country. Needless to say, the feedback, or training, session became central to the program, earning the name "T-group."[1]

Sadly, Lewin died before the first NTL session. But thanks to his "I sink ozzer," a powerful tool for research and social

[1]They were originally called "basic skills training groups," or BST groups, but there were too many wisecracks.

…ecame almost synony-
…ional change through small
…, its T-group format refused to stay home
…aine. It spread throughout North America under
…names, finally reaching the West Coast in time to become synonymous with "touchy-feely" nude marathons and the me-generation, a far cry indeed from the social-change goals of its birth.

However these groups were used, they were used. Carl Rogers (1968) called T-groups "the most significant social invention of this century." They have shown up in industry, education, family life, self-help organizations, and all the helping professions. Whatever they are called, the same principles tend to surface: feedback, hashing out misunderstandings, sticking to the here and now, reporting how other people's behavior makes one feel rather than prescribing how they ought to change, and supporting one another's attempts to try out new behaviors. Group members enter the hall of mirrors and, it is hoped, come out sensitive to what works when, with which people. And as for the training of social psychologists, T-groups taught many of them their first formal lessons on social influence, as the laboratory portion of courses in small-group process or interpersonal communications.

The Study of Interpersonal Communications and Group Processes

Imagine the excitement doctors must have felt when they first acquired the use of the X ray. T-groups created a similar situation for social psychologists—they had always been good at intuiting what was going on between people, but suddenly they were seeing so much more in these groups that were designed for that very purpose. With all these interactions being observed, there was a desire to do deeper research and test various hypotheses, and it became important to find some way to summarize and compare the goings-on during these hundreds and thousands of hours of group meetings. Thus a whole new interest arose in what later came to be called "interpersonal communication."

Robert Bales pioneered in this area, beginning as one of the members of the research team at the first Bethel workshops. The procedure he later formalized (Bales, 1950) as *Interaction Process Analysis* simply involved watching groups interact and, each time a person said something, noting who spoke to whom and the kind of thing said (for example, "asks for information," "gives suggestion," or "shows agreement"). In other words, every statement was categorized in various simple ways. Bales also collected information after the meeting on who liked whom (a technique developed much earlier by J.L. Moreno) and other questions, such as who the group thought was its leader.

This approach yielded interesting discoveries. For example, Bales, along with Philip Slater (Bales, 1958; Bales & Slater, 1955; Slater, 1955), used it to study discussion groups they had set up with the task of solving a fictional management problem and found, first off, that the person who speaks most is usually also the one who is most often spoken to. More interesting, this person is also likely to be the one who is seen by the other members as having "contributed the best ideas for solving the problem" and having done "the most to guide the discussion and keep it moving effectively." This same individual is also most likely to be rated by the members, after four sessions, as clearly being "the leader."

Yet this same person who ranked high on all those fine qualities was usually *not* the best-liked individual. Often this "task specialist" type of leader was the second most liked. But the best-liked member was called a "socioemotional specialist" by these researchers, because although he (all the participants were men) did not do much directly about getting the task done, he did the most to maintain group morale and harmony.

Also of interest was the fact that the two specialists tended to interact most with each other and to like each other more than they liked the other members of the group. Thus what Bales and Slater found is that a group spontaneously tends to find from among its members two people to play the roles of task and socioemotional specialists. They form a strong, internally cohesive coalition in the center of the group, much like parents in the traditional nuclear family.

Of course, not all groups are T-groups or specially constructed groups for laboratory experiments. In fact, the most important ones are the ongoing ones found in offices, classrooms, factories, and homes. And although certain basic structures, such as the two types of leaders, can usually be identified in any group, methods like Bales's can dig only so deep into "what's really going on" in a busy, buzzing, fighting, loving ongoing group. To sense more complex dynamics, a well-trained human brain, simply observing and thinking about what's going on, is still very useful. What is even more useful is if that socially sensitive, intuitive mind can then turn its vague insights into testable hypotheses that can be verified experimentally and thus made explicit enough for anyone to use in his or her group life. This ability to verbalize and scientifically verify the unverbalized in a group is what makes the socially aware social psychologist a useful scientist and not just a good party guest.

The Next Phase of Interpersonal Research—Nonverbal Communication, Specific Group Phenomena, and So On

The group dynamics movement—including T-groups, interpersonal communication research, and other small-group-oriented research—was the dominant force in social psychology from World War II through the 1950s. But by the late seventies, the most intense excitement about small groups had shifted to departments of business, education, and communications, where social psychology's innovative work with groups could be applied to the practical problems of these fields. Social psychology, meanwhile, became fascinated with attitude change and social "cognition." But social psychologists' interest in the subtleties of interpersonal relations did not evaporate; it simply broadened and left the T-group, in particular, behind.

One new line of research focused on nonverbal communication. We all respond, often unconsciously, to many nonverbal messages. But our social successes escalate dramatically when we become alert to the subtler nuances of nonverbal expression.

Suppose you are listening to someone give a talk. He sounds composed and assertive. But he's making some points you disagree with, and so you eagerly plan your response.

Now imagine that you take your mind off your own response long enough to watch him more closely. A trembling hand gives him away—this speaker is nervous. You notice a twitch at the corner of his mouth, too. Having made these additional observations, when you give your response you will probably begin by being supportive and reassuring (let's hope you don't use this knowledge to devastate the speaker). Quite possibly you will turn a potential adversary into an appreciative friend.

One often-quoted study (Mehrabian & Ferris, 1967) found that of all the information conveyed to another person when we say something that is emotional (not informational), only 7 percent is contained in the actual meaning of the words we use. We can also thank nonverbal cues for the fact that we can all get along as well as we do with people who do not speak our language.

The nonverbal "language" does vary from culture to culture, however. Consequently, it occasionally creates greater misunderstandings than verbal ignorance does, usually because people don't realize that there are differences across cultures in the meaning of certain gestures or facial expressions or of how far away one stands from the other when talking.

In our own culture, Marianne LaFrance and Clara Mayo (1976), social psychologists at Boston University, did a study comparing whites and blacks on the significance of looking the other person in the eye during conversations. They filmed one conversation of a black graduate student with a white executive and another conversation of the same graduate student with a black institutional administrator and laboriously analyzed the film, frame by frame, for who looked at whom and when. They also had teams of hidden observers watching two-person conversations at college cafeterias, fast-food restaurants, and hospital and airport waiting rooms.

The observers rigorously measures the amount of time each person looked in the other person's eyes when listening. They found that whites tend to look at others when listening but not when talking and that blacks tend to look at others when talking but not when listening. Thus whites and blacks easily misinterpret the messages they get when trying to know who should speak when. Reported the researchers:

> When the white listener . . . encountered a pause with sustained gaze from a black speaker, the white was cued to speak, and both found themselves talking at once. . . . By directing his gaze at the black listener, the white speaker often did not succeed in yielding the floor and had to resort to direct verbal questioning. (p. 551)

They note that such "miscues" and the necessity they may create for such things as direct questions "may lend an unintentionally confrontational tone to the encounter" (p. 551).

Even when intercultural differences are not an issue, people often get into trouble by ignoring the nonverbal message or by thinking they have gotten it when they haven't. For example, people give certain nonverbal cues that show when they are lying, such as speaking in a higher tone of voice (Zuckerman, DePaulo, & Rosenthal, 1981). Most people are not aware enough of these cues, however, to use them either to lie well or to detect lying. Instead they tend to focus on facial expression, which is easily controlled by the liar. Gerald Miller and Judee Burgoon (1982), in an article intended to help lawyers assess "witness credibility," reviewed all of the social psychology research literature then available on lying. They concluded from several different studies that while people are quite convinced they can tell when someone is lying, in most of the studies they do no better than chance.

Along with this continuing interest in interpersonal communication during the 1960s and 1970s was a steady interest in certain specific aspects of small-group interaction. For example, Bibb Latane (who conducted the seizure-and-helping studies described in chapter 1) arranged to have students yell as loudly as they could in a group but cleverly measured each person's volume independently (Latane, Williams, & Harkins, 1979). He found that people don't yell as loudly in a group as they will alone—a phenomenon he called "social loafing," which he related to the general impact that being in a group has on an individual's output or effort.

In fact, the interest in small-group phenomena continues to this day. For example, European social psychologists are particularly interested in what causes people to feel they are part of an in-group or an out-group. You will remember from chapter 1 that Muzafer Sherif and his colleagues were able to create in- and out-groups artificially by fostering competition between boys assigned arbitrarily to different cabins at a summer camp. This more recent research has found that it takes much less than that to create a distinction between in-group and out-group.

In one such study, done at New York University, Anne Locksley, Vilma Ortiz, and Christine Hepburn (1980) seated groups of six students in six separate cubicles where they could not see each other. The researchers then asked each student to pick lottery tickets out of a container the students believed held three "phi" tickets and three "gamma" tickets (these names were completely arbitrary). Each student was then asked to write down, privately, how many of a possible one hundred poker chips he or she would allocate to each of the other five students, who were identified only by whether they were phis or gammas. On the average, students allocated about eighty-five chips to each of the other members of their "own" group, whether phis or gammas, and only about sixty-five chips to each of the members of the "other" group. In a similar experiment, one also involving categorization into two "groups" based entirely on an arbitrary lottery, students consistently rated the members of the other group as being more self-centered, unfriendly, unreasonable, and unsportsmanlike, as well as *less* good natured, trustworthy, dependable, sincere, and considerate, than the members of their own group.

And the *Next* Phase: The Personal Relationships Movement

What we mean to illustrate in this chapter is that social psychologists' constant awareness of and interest in the face-to-face social interactions around them have been like a light reflected though many different prisms, many different phases of research interests. Alternatively, you could think of this interest as a scientific fire fueled by many different privately observed phenomena, in which case the newest, brightest blaze at the moment—a conflagration perhaps suited to the times—has been the study of personal relationships, including attraction, falling in love, and the ongoing intimacies of friendship, marriage, and family bonds.

The earliest major research effort that was at all relevant to close relationships was conducted mainly in the 1960s and involved the study of initial impressions of same-sex strangers. Then in the 1970s a few social psychologists began trying to research romantic attraction and love. At the same time, certain other researchers—especially those trained in groups or interpersonal communication—began to notice that families (including their own) are another kind of group, one that often needs help with its communications. By the end of the seventies, all these lines of research had continued and expanded.

Perhaps the most influential research program on marital communication was begun by John Gottman, first at the University of Illinois and now at the University of Washington. In a typical study, Gottman (1979) brought into his laboratory two types of couples: those who had sought marital counseling and also reported their marriages to be not so hot and those who had not sought counseling and were happy with their marriages. After years of preliminary observations, Gottman developed several interesting techniques. For example, he had couples discuss the perennial six o'clock question of "How was your day today, dear?" And some of his analysis of the responses was done by the couples themselves, whom Gottman seated at a table where they could push a lever backward or forward according to whether they were feeling good or bad as a result of what the other said.

With this simple device, Gottman verified some ideas that married couples can readily use. One is that the more negative the feelings produced by communications, the more likely is the relationship to be unhappy. Another is that happily married spouses are as likely to respond to a negative statement with a positive one as with a negative response; they don't escalate their negativities the way unhappy couples do. Overall, happy couples are less predictable in their responses. They don't have standard scripts that they rely on for getting by or that they turn to during conflicts. (This factor makes them harder to study but probably also makes them more interesting to be part of.)

Finally, as any "socially sensitive" social psychologist and his or her spouse can testify, the fact that someone knows the "right thing to say" is no guarantee it will always be said. Gottman found that spouses can watch another couple interact and know what to say to make the communication effective. But they do not necessarily use that skill with their own spouse.

Still, Howard Markman at the University of Denver found that teaching engaged couples the kinds of skills Gottman found to differentiate distressed from nondistressed couples does make a difference. In one study (Markman, Floyd, Stanley, & Storaasli, 1988) of twenty-one couples who had been randomly assigned to receive premarital communications training, only one had broken up by three years later, whereas five of the twenty-one control-group couples had broken up by that time. Moreover, of those couples who were still together three years later, the pairs who had received the premarital communications training were dramatically more satisfied and their problems much less intense in comparison with the control-group couples.

By 1980 the work on love, the research on family communications, and the other studies focusing on families and on long-term friendships were all rapidly coalescing into a significant new force in social psychology. And then it all came together: In 1982 the First International Conference on Personal Relationships was convened; in 1983 the book *Close Relationships,* written by a group of highly distinguished senior social psychologists, appeared; and in 1984 the first issue of the *Journal of Social and Personal Relationships* was published and the International Society for the Study of Personal Relationships founded.

All but one of these events (publication of *Close Relationships*) were masterminded by two researchers—Steve Duck and Robin Gilmour—who were in England at the time. As Duck put it, the success of his chosen field has been "rather like buying a house in a neighbourhood that suddenly becomes fashionable. It appears that many people in several different disciplines were waiting for some spark to set fire to their latent wishes to study the topic" (1988, p. xiv).

The 1982 international conference, organized by Duck and Gilmour, was a true landmark. There were about a hundred of us, including Gottman and Hatfield (whom we mentioned in chapter 1). Until that July we had all been working very much in isolation. Then suddenly we were together—in Madison, Wisconsin—for a feverish few days of exchanging ideas, comparing research methodologies, and, of course, forming personal relationships at high speed.

The research presentations included studies that have since become classics in this young field—for example, the research by Ladd Wheeler, Harry Reis, and John Nezlek (1983) conducted at the University of Rochester that involved students keeping a daily diary of their social interactions for two weeks, as well as answering a questionnaire on loneliness at the end of the two weeks. For both male and female students, the amount of time spent with males had no relation to a student's level of loneliness; however, the more time spent with females, the less the loneliness of both males *and* females.

Research on close relationships is continuing at a frantic pace today, with studies ranging from children's friendships to unobtrusive observation of what adults do when they first meet a stranger to the meaning of closeness in relationships that have lasted fifty years or more. One of our favorite recent studies was conducted by Cindy Hazan and Phil Shaver (1987). They arranged to have a questionnaire published in the *Rocky Mountain News* asking people about the kind of relationship they had had in childhood with their parents and about their current close relationships. As predicted by the researchers, the respondents' adult close relationships paralleled the three major patterns of infants' attachment to their mothers: securely attached, anxious/ambivalent, or avoidant.

At a recent conference on interpersonal relationships at Nags Head, South Carolina, where Bibb Latane and Deborah Richardson have been holding what we call "summer camp for social psychologists," Phil Shaver shared that his own personal relationships had led him to this research on kinds of attachments. And he was not alone—many of these researchers' presentations began or ended with such personal, real-life stories. And so Nags Head was one more reminder: Social psychologists experience their subject matter as tangible features of their lives.

In Conclusion: Reflections on This Hall of Mirrors

Social phenomena are the very fabric of most people's lives, including those of social psychologists. Accordingly, it is easy for social psychologists to see their theories and research come to life in everyday events and easy for everyday life to give rise to new theories and research.

But what about the idea that science should be objective—beyond the influence of one's personal life? Well, it sounds good in theory, but in practice it is, first, rarely the case and, second, probably rarely desirable. Long before B.F. Skinner became famous as a learning psychologist, he was excited and intrigued both by how circus animals are trained and by how various machines work—fascinations that served him in good stead later, as the developer of a rather mechanistic theory about learning. And while all the information necessary to arrive at the theory of evolution was available to a number of scientists at the time that Charles Darwin set sail on the *Beagle,* only Darwin was isolated on a ship with those ideas in his head (ideas he was personally quite attached to) and then exposed to a wide variety of species and ecologies, until his life situation almost forced the theory upon him.

In other words, it is often the interaction of a well-trained mind with its personal circumstances and even preferences that yields the best science.

Certainly, an objective attitude is the right goal for a scientist. But it is still personal interest that guides one into a particular field, determines the perspective from which one sorts out data, and motivates one to conduct one more experiment even after all energy is gone. It is the personal side that gets the juices flowing, and thus social psychology may be the lively science we have found it to be just because of this unusually intimate interaction between subjective experience and objective research.

4

"Emperor's New Clothes Are Highlight of Royal Festivities"

What Matters to Social Psychology Is What One Thinks One Sees

IN this chapter we turn to one of the central characteristics of the content of social psychology: its long-standing position that people's *experience* of their world is more important than the objective features of that world. Does this sound dull? You'd be surprised, for in this chapter we are going to report on what is as close to an all-out war as ever happens in science.

Throw certain pieces of paper $2\frac{5}{8}'' \times 6\frac{1}{8}''$ out of a car on a freeway and Americans, at least, will scream a word that sounds like "money" and risk their lives collecting the stuff. Indians from the jungles of Brazil, however, would no doubt behave quite "sensibly" in this situation, having no experience with the stuff—no *social* experience, of hearing their parents arguing over it, of exchanging it with other people for various goodies, of seeing people on TV kill for it.

Given that the Indians from Brazil would have essentially the same brains and see the very same scene, it must be that somewhere inside they would be *thinking* differently about those pieces of paper thrown from the car. That is probably a completely obvious point. And if you were to pick up an introductory psychology textbook today and turn to the first chapter, chances are you would find psychology defined as the "study of behavior and mental processes." Ten years ago, however, the words *and mental processes* would have been missing. That's right. Their omission for years and now their recent reappearance represent not one but two hard-fought revolutions in psychology.

The first revolution was fought to make psychology strictly the study of behavior—no speculation or introspection. The second was fought to overthrow the tyranny of the first and to reopen psychology to the study of cognition. Mental processes. Thinking. And when we say these changes were each revolutions, we mean revolutions—ones in which people nearly came to blows.

In the period in which social psychology grew up as a science, the 1930s through the 1950s, the dominant perspective in American psychology was *behaviorism.* You have probably heard before of this view that if psychology is going to be scientific, psychologists must limit their data to the quantification of behavior, in particular the probabilities of seeing certain responses given that certain stimuli are present. Stimuli and responses, situations and behaviors—these can be reliably observed by anyone at any time. Thoughts, feelings, motivations—these can be observed only by the person having them. According to behaviorists, it is impossible to know if, for example, when I say I feel happy, I am referring to the same internal state as you experience when you say it. Behaviorists are famous for their opinion that the mind should be treated as a "black box": What goes in and goes out is a valid topic for science, but what goes on inside the walls of that magical box is beyond our ken.

Behaviorism swept psychology, beginning in 1913 with John Watson's "Psychology as the Behaviorist Views It." It is hard to fathom now the intensity of this movement. It was a reaction to "experimental introspection," a methodology that seems now to have been hopelessly flawed, yet it was the main approach of psychology when Watson was a graduate student, around

1900. At that time psychology was defined as the study of human consciousness. But the new generation was having its doubts, Watson especially.

Geiwitz and Moursund (1979) claim that Watson "was uncomfortable using human subjects; he was shy, embarrassed, and awkward. He was more comfortable with animals" (p. 94). So he taught a rat to run a maze and wrote a paper, in the style of the day, trying to interpret his observations in terms of the rat's consciousness, ending his sentences frequently with "if the rat has consciousness at all."

Not surprisingly, he got sick of the whole approach and in 1913 changed psychology forever with these opening four sentences of his paper:

> Psychology as the behaviorist views it is a purely objective experimental branch of natural science. Its theoretical goal is the prediction and control of behavior. Introspection forms no essential part of its methods, nor is the scientific value of its data dependent upon the readiness with which they lend themselves to interpretation in terms of consciousness. The behaviorist, in his efforts to get a unitary scheme of animal response, recognizes no dividing line between man and brute. (p. 158)

Almost every specialization within psychology accepted Watson's argument, bowing down under the relentless criticism of the young, radical followers of Watson.[1] Only social psychology held out. Social psychologists, almost without exception, continued to focus on the inner experience of people. They usually were not shy and they certainly did not prefer to work with animals.

Thanks to this "heroic legacy," a haven was maintained

---

[1]Besides being shy, in his youth Watson is said by Schultz (1975) to have been "indolent, argumentative, and not easily controlled." He fought a great deal and was twice arrested, once for shooting firearms inside the city limits of his hometown. While attending the University of Chicago he found the famous John Dewey "incomprehensible." Later, his career of turning psychology upside down was abruptly ended by his affair with a laboratory assistant, which led to a highly publicized divorce and his resignation from Johns Hopkins University. He went on to make a fortune in advertising, where he "did things in great style and loved to show a display of power" (Larson and Sullivan, p. 352, quoted in Schultz). All in all, he is an easy person to cast as a semivillain or a romantic outlaw!

within psychology for those who wanted to research internal processes. In particular, one important distinction was preserved and elaborated on: There is a difference between what happens to people (the behaviorist's "stimuli") and how people *experience* what happens to them. And if you want to understand what people will do (the behaviorist's "response"), the crucial thing to understand in any research is not what the experimenter observed but what the *subject* observed. This is termed a *phenomenological* emphasis, and it was vehemently opposed by behaviorism.[2]

The importance of this distinction between external events and the internal experience of them has been accepted as almost an article of faith by social psychologists, even during the dark years of behaviorism. When we raised the issue with various social psychologists, most of them huffily replied that "of course" social psychology had always been "cognitive." And people-based, not rat-based. But then several who had been social psychologists in the behaviorist years of psychology admitted that it had been hard to be the only dissenters. As Jerry Singer said, "We took a beating" for it. Several even used the same phrase: "We were carrying the torch." And John Arrowood spoke of the "loneliness" of being the only faculty member on the hall holding such an outrageous position.

The position was held nonetheless. Then, around 1970, it became less lonely, as psychology finally threw off its behavioristic shackles and became largely "cognitive"—an emancipation that many social psychologists believe was due in part to the courageous rebelliousness of some of their own, such as Jerome Bruner. Bruner, originally a social psychologist, became a founder of the new movement within general psychology, in which objective experimental methods of studying behavior were used to make precise inferences about issues of how people think and remember.

---

[2]On one point, all of psychology did capitulate and rightly so: that we can never know for sure what has gone on inside a mind, especially if it is not our own. We can observe only behavior and situations. But social psychologists generally believe there is no reason they can't use their observations to infer what went on mentally. In fact, not to try to make these inferences tends to make us poorer predictors of behavior, as well as students of the trivial.

Why They Held Their Ground

We have to admit that not absolutely all social psychologists eschewed behaviorism—a position so very consistent with the long-standing American emphasis on the observable world and practical affairs, not vague thoughts and theories.[3]

But the general position was provided, once again, by Kurt Lewin. He had been part of the Gestalt revolution in Germany, which emphasized holistic perceptual and mental processes. Gestalt psychology and behaviorism were actually both revolts against psychology as it had begun, in Europe. The purpose of early psychology's method of introspection—the method behaviorists so disliked—was to analyze mental processes into their smallest discrete units, like mental atoms. Although the behaviorists did like this idea of discrete units, they said the right little units were stimulus-response bonds. The Gestalt psychologists, by contrast, were quite comfortable with a psychology that emphasized mental processes (even if they had to improve on its original methods a little) but totally rejected the breaking down of experience into little units. In other words, Gestalt and behaviorist psychologists could hardly have disagreed more.

Gestalt psychology, by claiming that mental processes such as perception, learning, and memory involved irreducible wholes instead of the accretion of tiny parts, had been a "loyal opposition" within European psychology for several decades. In Europe, academics had fought for their view on this issue with tremendous vehemence. Students of some professors holding one view could not even be seen in the company of professors from the other camp. Thus, Kurt Lewin was used to this sort of furor. When he got to the United States and found behaviorism taking over, he was not about to give up studying the mind, or social perception, or social groups—or to stop thinking of these as wholes—just because some funny guy from North Carolina with a fondness for rats said it was not to his taste.

---

[3]One such exception is Daryl Bem, who describes himself as a bit of a loner. You'll learn more about this interesting character in chapter 6. Bem came to social psychology via physics and says he "never had a mentor" in the usual, traditional sense of social psychology—so he has an excuse.

Not only did Lewin believe it was important to know how people perceive and think, but he really saw the observable world of stimuli and behaviors to be of only secondary importance. His reality was the "life space" of all the forces, ideas, memories, desires, and so forth that influenced a person at each moment in time. This was a mental world. Unless the individual was *aware* of some "objective fact," it had no impact on the life space. Even a person's past subjective experience did not matter, except as it was represented by current memories.[4]

Lewin's vision of the life space was his trademark even more than his Quasselstrippe, which we described in previous chapters. During every lecture he drew the oval life-space diagram on the blackboard, or on a napkin, or in the dust, whatever was handy. Fritz Heider recalls that the first time Lewin spoke to him about the life space was on a cold winter evening in Berlin while they were waiting for a tram:

> He used the tip of his umbrella to trace a small circle enclosed by a larger oval on the snow-covered pavement. He explained that these figures represented the person within his own life space. Then he drew a little plus sign within the oval—that was the person's goal—and a line separating the person from the goal, which was the barrier. Thus he was able to represent many situations by means of [these diagrams]. (1983, p. 79)

One psychologist recalls that when Lewin would have the Quasselstrippe meetings at home, the floor would be covered with sheets of brown wrapping paper, which those attending would use for diagraming the life space: "The 'full-fledged topologists' came to these sessions equipped with four-color pen-

---

[4]Lewin first thought of the life space when he was a soldier during World War I. War was as traumatic for him as anyone, but he was fascinated by his own responses to it. He wrote an article entitled "The War Landscape," in which he described how a landscape is perceived as open and without direction in peace, but in war, as the soldier proceeds toward the front lines, he sees the landscape in terms of favorable positions for defending himself and places where food and shelter might be had and as having a front and back, boundaries and zones. Objects in a battle zone become the soldier's property not because he fought for them but because the soldier sees everything as existing for military purposes. Prior to World War I, Lewin had actually done considerable research on associationism. But he gave it up around 1917, certain that a major modification in theory was needed, no doubt in part because of these experiences (Marrow, 1969).

cils, to squat on their hands and knees and draw on wrapping paper" (Marrow, 1969, p. 89).

Lewin's students irreverently called these ovals "little eggs." By the time Lewin's students' students got to them, they had grown into "bathtubs." Until well after Lewin's death in 1947, they were a trademark almost as much of social psychology as of Lewin. And although life-space diagrams are no longer in fashion, the basic view of the mind as the essential reality continues to flourish and to spread, in spite of the temporary wet blanket tossed on by behaviorism. In social psychology, study after study has distinguished and will probably continue to distinguish between the situation as it is and the situation as the individual perceives and interprets it. It is as though every social psychologist has, watching over his or her shoulder, not Watson but Lewin, who made his point eloquently and for all time when he said:

> To describe a situation "objectively" in psychology actually means to describe the situation as a totality of those facts and only those facts which make up the field of that individual. To substitute for that world of the individual the world of the teacher, of the physicist, or of anybody else is to be, not objective, but wrong. (1942/1951a, p. 62)

It would be inaccurate to overemphasize Lewin's contribution on this point, however. Other pioneering social psychologists were just as adamant. Ted Newcomb said, "It seems to me to be a truism that no interpersonal behavior can be understood without a knowledge of how the relationship is perceived by the persons involved" (1947, p. 74). And Solomon Asch—who, like Lewin, studied with the Gestaltists—said, "It is not possible, as a rule, to conduct investigations in social psychology without including a reference to the experience of persons" (1959, p. 374).

When every other field within psychology became so vehemently opposed to the study of the thinking process, why did Lewin, Newcomb, Asch, and nearly every other social psychologist insist on this heresy? A lot of it seemed to have to do with the strong interest in the study of the formation and development of measures of attitudes. During most of the behaviorist years of general psychology, the bulk of social psychology was focused on attitudes, a very mental kind of thing. And why were attitudes so important to early social psychologists? Robert Zajonc (1980) thinks the emphasis was yet another part of their reaction to the rise of nazism.

> American social psychologists asked themselves how it was possible for a nation like Germany, with one of the richest [cultural] . . . traditions, to change so rapidly . . . to tolerate the obliteration of . . . humanitarian . . . values. Germany was viewed as the product of a massive attitude change—a massive *cognitive* change—which was achieved by means of extremely effective propaganda.
>
> If political, economic, and social changes of unequaled scope can take place by virtue of persuasion . . . the role of cognitive processes in social life must be exceedingly important. How then could a social psychologist be anything but cognitive? (p. 189)

Lewin's most famous student, Leon Festinger, whom you will meet in chapter 6, explained it quite simply: "From the point of view of understanding humans, if you look at nothing but behavior, you're ignoring a vast world that exists for human beings. . . . [If] you're concerned with creating a change in behavior that lasts and endures . . . something has to have gone on inside the person" (Festinger quoted in Evans, 1980, pp. 132–33).

And there may be one other reason. We have already discussed it: chutzpah. Social psychologists seem to enjoy shaking up the status quo. It was hard being cognitive in an era of entrenched, self-satisfied behaviorism. But it was also fun, and revolutionary. Perhaps for the radicals who began social psychology, it would have been harder to go along with the stuffy experimentalists down the hall than to fight them. In that sense, they followed exactly in Watson's boots.

Social Perception, Attribution Theory, and Social Cognition

For whatever reason, social psychology has been and is emphatically cognitive. And it obviously sided with the victors—

those who wanted to add the study of "mental processes" to the definition of psychology. Today not just social psychology but nearly all of psychology is thoroughly cognitive. Behavior remains the only thing that can actually be measured, of course, but the objects of study are now frequently internal states, structures, and processes. And "behavior" includes, for example, answering questions about what one is feeling or thinking. Unlike in the days of introspection, however, it is now understood (ideally) that asking such questions only gives a researcher some idea of what subjects have chosen to report about what they believe they were thinking or feeling. Thus many other ingenious ways of deducing these inner mental processes have been developed. The important point is that it is now generally accepted that to ignore these mental processes throws out too many babies with their bath waters.

Perhaps because of the constant need in the past to demonstrate the impact of inner realities on behavior, a great deal of social psychology's cognitive research has focused on discrepancies between external, observable reality and one's internal reality. We began this chapter with one example: The external, observable reality of money lying in the street is that *colored paper* is lying on the street. "Money" is an interpretation we give to what we see, based on our social experience. More interesting examples occur, of course, when we lack, choose to ignore, or for experimental purposes are deluded about objective information (for example, during the Asch conformity experiments described in chapter 2).

Or consider these examples. In the area of stress on the job, the same amount of noise has fewer stressful effects if workers *believe* they have control over it (Glass & Singer, 1972). And in the case of helping behavior, how likely people are to come to the aid of an injured person mainly depends on whether they *perceive* the person to be injured, whether they *consider* it their responsibility to help, and whether they *think* of themselves as capable of helping (Latane & Darley, 1970).

In almost every area of social psychology, the distinction between actual and perceived has been central. In fact, several areas focus exactly on that. These areas are known by such names as "social perception," "attribution theory," and, most recently, "social cognition," the current dominant movement in social psychology. But let's stay historical: First, let us consider the grandparent of social cognition, the study of *impression formation*—a part of social perception that is now an old-timer, as topics go, but is still going strong. Solomon Asch (1946), with his strong Gestalt background and interest in perceptual processes, started what became the modern study of social perception. Right after World War II he did a study that found that if you ask people to form an impression of another person based on a list of descriptive terms, such as *warm, polite, honest,* and *busy,* people do not give these terms equal weight as they form their impression. Certain terms, such as *warm* or *cold,* contribute more to the impression—they are "central traits"—than such "peripheral" terms as *polite* or *honest.* On the battlefield against behaviorism, this finding was evidence that people do not passively respond to external stimuli. They reorganize information, putting some ahead of others. (And this process goes on inside a *mind,* not a black box.)

Next, let us introduce you to Harold Kelley, who took Asch's ideas further. Kelley became interested in social psychology while he was an undergraduate at Berkeley. During World War II he worked with the social psychologist Stuart Cook on a study of personnel selection for the armed forces. After the war, Cook went to New York to work on a project of Lewin's, and in the process, Kelley got to know Lewin and became his student. Many consider Kelley the greatest social psychologist still working today. He is certainly considered one of the nicest—and "nice" in the Lewinian tradition. Jerry Singer, once Kelley's student, reports that Kelley

> used to run sessions at his house over a series of weekends where he'd invite small groups of graduate students, his and everybody else's, just to spend an evening so that they'd get to know each other and have a cohesive groups. He really cared about people.

John Arrowood, also one of Kelley's former students, said, "He was a gentleman . . . we all knew that if there was anything that was bothering us, having to do with our academic or other research work, his door was always open."

One of Kelley's first studies (1950) examined how Asch's central-trait idea affected impressions of actual people. Kelley told students in three classes at MIT that their professor could not come for the day but that a guest lecturer would take his place and that he, Kelley, would like the students to evaluate the lecturer's performance afterward. The students received a note telling them a little about the instructor they would have—about his teaching experience, academic background, age, marital status, and such. For half the students, the note ended this way: "People who know him consider him to be a rather cold person, industrious, critical, practical, and determined." The other half received notes identical except that the words *very warm* were substituted for *rather cold.*

The results were clear. During the class session, 56 percent of the subjects with the "warm" description participated in the discussion, while only 32 percent of subjects receiving the "cold" description did so. And on ratings of the instructor completed after class, the "warm" instructor was consistently rated more positively.

In his introduction to the study, Kelley wrote that it was based on Asch's work, in which "it proved to be necessary to postulate inner-observer variables which contribute to the impression and which remain relatively constant through time." Take that, John Watson.[5]

Kelley's work was followed by many other studies on impression formation. Soon the topic's social relevance had expanded it into the study of stereotypes. Social psychologists wanted to know how distorted impressions were formed of, for example, racial or ethnic groups, men and women, or older people. This

[5]At some point we must be fair to Watson, Skinner, and all the rest. *In theory,* behaviorism can probably explain anything without any reference to internal states, even if a cognitive approach seems more sensible. We merely need to know the entire conditioning history of each individual. If a person reacts to the word *warm* or makes jokes about some ethnic group, he or she has been reinforced for this behavior in the past or these responses as associated with certain stimuli. Words can be stimuli. Reinforcers can be social (by being "secondary," so that if we associate laughter with mother, and mother with food, then if someone laughs at our ethnic joke, we are being reinforced). Even our own thoughts can reinforce us in modern behavioral theories. But the whole construction got so complicated—and the behaviorists had ruled the roost for so long, with so little graciousness—that at some point it was easier to start over rather than continue to remodel the old coop.

interest continues to the present. One fascinating, sophisticated example is a study by John Darley and Paget Gross (1983).

You may remember Darley as one of the researchers with Bibb Latane in the study of bystander intervention described in chapter 1. Darley was strongly influenced later by Solomon Asch, among others. But the interesting thing about Darley was that, as a child, he knew Asch, Festinger, Kelley, Schachter, and all the other "greats." Darley's father was chairman of the psychology department at the University of Minnesota during the era when everyone who was anyone at all in social psychology was, just had been, or soon would be a student or on the faculty. Darley reports: "I remember listening to their discussion in our living room. . . . Much of what I do . . . comes directly from those teachers" (quoted in Evans, 1980, p. 215).

Darley is now a professor of psychology at Princeton, where, with Paget Gross, then a student, he looked more deeply at how stereotypes affect the information we use in making decisions about people. To put it in the enemy's terms, Darley and Gross examined how stimuli go into the black box and different behaviors come out, *depending* on the intervening thought processes.

College students were shown one of two videotapes of a pretty, blonde fourth-grader named Hannah.[6] Students were randomly assigned to see one or the other of the tapes. Both tapes began with a four-minute segment of scenes of Hannah at a playground and around her neighborhood and school. One tape showed Hannah in a "stark fenced-in school yard" and "in an urban setting of rundown two-family homes." Her school was "a three-story brick structure set close to the street, with an adjacent asphalt school yard" (p. 23). In the other tape, Hannah was "playing in a tree-lined park," lived in an upper-middle-class suburban neighborhood, and attended a modern, sprawling school with playing fields and "a shaded playground." The col-

[6]Was this choice of name an unconscious tribute to Kurt Lewin? Darley told us he did not recall the following connection. But Lewin's popularity in the United States began when he attended the 1929 meeting of the American Psychological Association. Although he spoke little English, his tremendous enthusiasm about social psychology impressed even those who could not understand his German. Also impressive, apparently, was a film he brought along of a toddler. The film demonstrated his principle of forces in a field, and the little girl's name was Hannah.

lege students also got a "fact sheet" about Hannah, stating that she was in the fourth grade and other basic information. All of this was the same for all subjects, except that those who saw the "poor" Hannah were told her parents had had only a high school education and now her father was a meat packer and her mother a seamstress. In the other condition, Hannah's parents were both college graduates—an attorney and a freelance writer.

On the basis of the tape, *half* the college students in *each* tape-viewing condition were asked to make an evaluation of Hannah's grade-level ability in various school subjects.

Surprise! Seeing the tapes seemed to have no effect: Students from both groups rated the girl at about the fourth-grade level in all the different subjects. In fact, many of the students very rationally refused to make a rating at all, saying they did not have enough information.

But here is where the study gets interesting. Darley and Gross then showed the remaining half of the students in each group another twelve minutes of videotape. This time they saw Hannah completing a school achievement test on which they could see both the questions and her answers to them, about two-thirds of which were correct. All the college students saw exactly the same tape for this part of the experiment.

When *these* students were asked to rate Hannah's grade level on various subjects, suddenly their responses showed the effect of seeing one or the other of the two previous tapes. Those who had seen a "poor" Hannah said she showed low ability; those who had seen an "affluent" Hannah credited her with abilities that were a grade level higher.

What happened? From other questions about the ratings, Darley and Gross found that the viewers did form a hypothesis about Hannah based on their initial impression but were unwilling to act on that hypothesis without more information. Yet the subsequent objective information was not used objectively; it was used to confirm the hypothesis. Those subjects who thought Hannah was a child of the upper class saw the test she took as more difficult, remembered her as answering more items correctly, and recalled more positive behaviors, such as paying close attention to questions, and fewer negative behaviors, such as staring off into space. The opposite was true of those who thought she came from a lower-class background.

The study has many messages, both theoretical and practical. For this chapter's purposes, it is enough to point out again that this kind of research requires a focus on subjective experience. True, certain "stimuli" have certain "associations," but that is about all that can easily be said of this study from a behaviorist's point of view. Nor would a behaviorist probably have done such a study, given the impossibility of knowing the conditioning history of the subjects. The only way to know that history would be to control it—to raise some human subjects isolated from all social influences until exposing them to the experimental stimulus. And that would undoubtedly have such a devastating effect on the subjects that it would be an utterly unethical experiment.

Attribution Theory: Part I
Flighty Fritz and His Film of Flitting Forms

The most influential theoretical perspective in social psychology for the past twenty years or so has been *attribution theory.* It says that people do not just passively observe but spontaneously evaluate and attribute causes for what they see, especially if what they are seeing is another person.

For example, if a friend forgets your birthday, do you simply observe the nonevent and let it go? No, if you are like most of us, you attribute the forgetting to your friend's being thoughtless or very busy right now or secretly planning a surprise party for you. We humans are such full-time attributors, especially of social events, that it is a wonder social psychology didn't begin with this topic.

Actually, it practically did. But the man who was first interested in attribution was such a laid-back fellow that it took him a few decades to write the seminal book. And it took a couple of more decades for anyone to notice it, since Fritz Heider was not the charismatic sort. But in time his book became number one on everyone's list.

Fritz Heider was a close friend of Lewin's from the start, but they were very different types. Fritz grew up in Austria, the son of a well-to-do architect and amateur archaeologist (for an account of his life, see Heider, 1983). And Fritz himself had a reputation for being a flighty dilettante.

He wasn't lazy; he just couldn't settle onto one project for life. He began studying architecture, then switched to law, then to philosophy and psychology. But this chronology only begins to capture the variety of his interests. His autobiography tells of an endless round of studying this and that, here and there, during an "extended adolescence." He took trips to Italy at whim and to Berlin for years at a time. He had countless jobs, from installing burglar alarms to teaching at an orphanage. Lewin tried to help him with a job making lampshades; Fritz lasted for four shades. His parents were delighted and amazed when he earned his doctorate (he wrote that he did it mainly because everyone else was getting one and it seemed easy).

His wanderlust, however, became a saving characteristic when it made him say yes on a moment's notice to a suggestion that he go to the United States to work in a psychology laboratory at a school for the deaf (with the famous Gestalt psychologist Kurt Koffka). As a result, Heider was out of Germany when Hitler rose to power and in a position to help others, like Lewin, make their move when it became necessary.

In Northampton, Massachusetts, in the laboratory at the school for the deaf, Heider met Grace Moore. With his typical lack of hesitation, Heider plunged into the relationship and the couple married three months later. Grace proved to be the necessary ballast; the two stayed married. And they have moved only once since, from Northampton, where Heider eventually taught at Smith College, to the University of Kansas at Lawrence.

Lewin, in contrast, was the son of a middle-class shopkeeper. The Lewins were Jews in East Prussia, and so Kurt knew all about prejudice and hard times. He worked hard at his education and knew exactly what he wanted—an academic position, even though as a Jew he knew that a good position with tenure was impossible. Also unlike Heider, Lewin stayed put in Berlin, and it was emotionally very difficult for him to emigrate when it became necessary. Lewin was relentlessly extroverted and social; Fritz Heider was more of an introvert. Lewin was also something of a type A personality, with hundreds of projects going on at once; it took Fritz years to produce his few books. As a result, perhaps, Lewin died of a heart attack when he was fifty-seven, and Fritz finished his autobiography in 1983 at the age of eighty-seven.

The tortoise takes his time, but his accomplishments may become legendary. This is especially true in the case of Heider. He was an observer at the periphery for a long time, taking up Lewin's ideas; those of Henry Murray, a personality psychologist; and even those of Clark Hull, a learning psychologist. But he abandoned these ideas when they didn't help him understand his particular interest, interpersonal relations. Harold Kelley says that his own impression of Heider was like everyone's: "He was a dreamy, thoughtful, converted-artist, aesthetic kind of person—doing these very off-the-wall, out-of-the-field things. Then they'd turn out finally to be exceedingly important."

The birth of attribution theory is the best example of what Kelley is talking about. It seems that Heider wanted to understand how people's commonsense observations of others affect their relationships. With his student Marianne Simmel (see Heider & Simmel, 1944), he made a film of geometric forms and showed them to people. (He had used the same forms at the school for the deaf to study puzzle-solving.) He found that everyone watching films of these shapes moving around would, quite spontaneously, describe the action in terms of people: The triangles were men, the circles were women, they fought, loved, had happy reunions, got in and out of balance with each other, and so forth. The universality of these perceptions was quite astounding.

These *attributions* were the beginning of attribution theory. If people attributed so much to mere objects, Heider reasoned, they must attribute much more to people. From that insight he developed his now-famous ideas.

Attribution Theory: Part II
Of Nudes and Quiz Shows

Although Heider began to write about attribution around 1944, the theory did not meander into the mainstream of social psychology until the mid-1960s, when it was revived simultaneously by several researchers. Of these, E.E. "Ned" Jones and Hal Kelley made the most influential contributions.

Ned Jones recalls that when he first saw the Heider and Simmel film of moving geometric shapes, "I thought it was kind of dumb." But Jones was at Harvard, and a researcher there, John Thibaut (a Lewin student, of course) got Jones actually to read one of Heider's papers—"an extremely important experience for me." Then another Harvard faculty member, Jerome Bruner—that social psychologist who practically invented cognitive psychology—pointed out to Jones the work of Solomon Asch on social perception. These two influences combined with Jones's own ideas to produce a paper (coauthored with Keith Davis, Jones's student at the time) that began a revolution in social psychology—"From Acts to Dispositions: The Attribution Process in Person Perception" (Jones and Davis, 1965).

Of course, it may also be that the time was ripe for this kind of thinking, for at almost exactly the same time another major social psychologist, also influenced by Asch and Heider, came up with almost the same idea. That was Hal Kelley, who earlier had conducted the experimental test of Asch's "warm-cold" findings on impression formation. And again, it was Kelley's exposure to Heider's ideas that made the difference.

Kelley told us that at the University of Minnesota the faculty held regular meetings at which they would report on various books they had agreed to read for the group's information. Kelley acquiesced to reading Heider's (1958) book, a work that he says he certainly would never have looked at with much care had he not been obliged to. He liked the book so much, however, that he wrote a paper on attribution for the Nebraska Symposium on Motivation (Kelley, 1967). In it he took Heider's fairly general notions and put them in terms that were not only easy to test experimentally but also related to social psychologists' own experience as researchers. Phil Shaver, speaking from the perspective of more than twenty years later, describes Kelley's rethinking of Heider as the foremost example of a contribution that actually "restructured the way people think about things."

In the mid-1960s, when the Kelley and Jones papers appeared, the major social psychology journals reported virtually no research on the topic of attributions, or how people explain the behavior of themselves and others. Ten years later, one in every twelve articles was explicitly concerned with attribution theory (Lamberth, 1980) and a great many of the others made reference to it in their discussion of results. Attribution theory had become the major thread of social psychology theory.

Again, what is central to attribution theory is the distinction it makes between what is actual and what people perceive to be the case. This distinction is important in understanding people's attributions about both others and themselves. For example, with regard to attributions people make about themselves, Stuart Valins (1966) asked male college students to look at slides in order to judge the attractiveness of ten different nude women depicted in the slides. As the subjects were seeing the pictures, one at a time, they were also listening through earphones to what they thought was their heart rate. When the experimenters made the "heart rate" increase during a particular slide, that slide was rated as more attractive. And when the subjects were given the opportunity to take some of the slides home with them, those were the slides they selected. Clearly, the subjects attributed their (supposed) increased heart rates to their attraction to the slide. (More precisely, Valins suggests that when they heard their own "heartbeat" increase, they looked closely at the slide to "confirm" their hypothesis that the picture was in fact more arousing.)

Given that a person's subjective attributions of the cause of an event are more important than what objectively caused it, the next issue is what determines these attributions. This question is mainly asked regarding how people explain the causes of others' behavior; one of the most important answers came from Lee Ross.

Ross, originally a student of Stanley Schachter's and now a professor of social psychology at Stanford, first gave a name to a "phenomenon long familiar to social psychologists in the Lewinian tradition"—the *fundamental attribution error.* This phrase refers to the tendency of people to explain other people's actions as due to personality characteristics rather than the situation, no matter how inappropriate. For example, if someone lies, we tend to say that person is dishonest, whatever the social pressure he or she was under.

Ross became aware of the fundamental attribution error, he told us, at the oral examinations of two doctoral candidates. At the first, his own examination, he recalls that he felt in great awe of the important scholars who were examining him. They seemed to have so much more knowledge and ability than he. But one year later he was a professor examining a doctoral student, and although he had not learned that much in one year, he realized that the student saw him as an important scholar with much more knowledge and ability. The professors saw one another that way, too. Everybody was making the attribution error—seeing others in terms of personal characteristics when the only important difference was their relative social positions, which had been emphasized by their roles at the examination.

Thus Lee Ross and two of his students, Teresa Amabile and Julia Steinmetz (1977), conducted what has become a famous attribution study. Pairs of college students who did not know each other participated in the experiment. When they arrived, one of each pair was arbitrarily designated the "questioner" and the other the "contestant" in a "quiz show game." The questioners were asked first to make up ten fairly difficult questions to which they happened to know the answers and then to ask them. On the average, the contestants could answer about six.

At the end of the experiment, each participant was asked to rate the other's "general knowledge"—not the specific knowledge the questions were on. In almost every case, the contestants thought the questioners were more *generally* knowledgeable than they themselves. Even uninvolved observers tended to make the same judgments. While everyone was aware that the questioner had the advantage in asking questions to which the questioner happened to know the answers, the difference was perceived as due to personal characteristics.

This distinction is not just some abstract principle. Think about how much difference it makes, for example, if a husband is upset by something his wife has done and, although in fact the action was necessitated by circumstances, he sees it as another instance of her fundamental "carelessness" or "lack of consideration." One social psychologist, in fact, explained that he first became aware of the operation of the fundamental attribution error in his life when he noticed that even though his wife was at least as knowledgeable and intelligent as his eminent male colleagues, they saw her as less so, probably because women are taught not to exert control over what is talked about in a discussion. But this difference was perceived by his male colleagues as a personal characteristic—that she knew less!

Social Cognition and the Ultimate Study of the Importance of Subjective Reality

Now that social psychology has seen its cognitive approach become acceptable, it has been free to go beyond merely demonstrating the importance of inner realities by comparing them with outer realities. It has begun to explore the actual structure and processes of what is now called "social cognition." A prime example is the work of Abraham Tesser at the University of Georgia.

Abe Tesser—a slight, bright-eyed, enthusiastic lover of new ideas and clever research—was always fond of a certain set of brilliant studies about "group polarization." In these studies, David Myers (for example, 1982) and other researchers demonstrated that after a group has discussed a controversial issue, the average of the group members' individual views will shift to become a more extreme version of the initial pro or con direction of the average. And Abe, as a firm believer in the reality and influence of mental processes, wondered if this process of polarization in groups might happen in people's minds as well, without any group to discuss the issue with. That is, if you have an opinion about something and then have a chance merely to think more about it, instead of becoming more moderate in your opinion, could your original viewpoint shift to a more extreme position? Could this happen just by thinking about an issue, on your own?

To see, Tesser conducted a simple experiment. On each of several issues, subjects were first asked to indicate how much they agreed or disagreed with a statement such as "In many cases, revolution is the best way to correct political and social problems" (Tesser, 1978, p. 299). They were then given a few seconds to think about the statement and asked to rate their agreement or disagreement again. Of those given thirty seconds to think, about 25 percent gave more emphatic ratings, compared with their original feeling. Of those given two minutes to think, 65 percent became more emphatic.

Tesser and his students and colleagues have conducted a series of such studies on a range of topics, from opinions on social issues to impressions of people. In each case, as Tesser concludes, "simply thinking about some object can result in attitude change" (p. 304). This all comes about, he explains, because when we think about something, other associated mental structures get connected up and add to the original thought's significance. The mental world is a powerful kingdom.

Tesser said of his work:

> Underlying much of the idea of self-generated attitude change is the notion that the world is really a construction and these [mental structures] help us to construct it. Without the [mental] structures], there is no construction. If there's no construction, there's no change.

In a general way, everything we have talked about in this chapter is the study of "social cognition." But the phrase is mainly used in a more restricted way, to refer to studies like Tesser's that emphasize the structure and dynamics of the inner processes themselves. Other research in social cognition looks at memory and speed of processing information, yielding new insights about such long-standing social psychology topics as stereotypes, the self-concept, and attitudes.

Ten years ago, social cognition was only one of several lively lines of work in social psychology; these days, it has captured center stage. The growth gave its leaders some exciting times, as Susan Fiske recalls. She, along with Shelly Taylor, wrote *Social Cognition*, a cornerstone volume of the new movement. Fiske told us the following:

> You were seeing just how far you could push a cognitive account. It was like a dare—how far could you push it. For example,

> stereotyping—it was studied for years and years and years by very smart people. The challenge was whether you could find something new—find stereotyping is not motivational, not restricted to people who are pathological, not merely part of an authoritarian personality. Stereotyping might be part of people's normal cognitive processes. Gordon Allport had said it, but no one had researched it much. That was part of it, too—methodology was exciting, too. Because it was hard. Precise and difficult measures, yet with real social stimuli. Could you do it? And in a bridge discipline [between social and cognitive psychology] there's always the risk you'll fall into the ravine in between.

What is the difference between social cognition and cognitive psychology generally? Mainly that social psychology's version of cognition focuses on the real world—how people perceive others, how others' perceptions affect them. Nor does social cognition ignore what people feel. Thus one social psychologist we spoke with characterized the "other" cognitive psychology as "juiceless"—and started to say "useless" as well, before correcting herself!

That's okay. We should have expected that social psychology's study of cognition would be especially spirited.

In Conclusion: Are We Now Rebels without a Cause?

Are you wondering yet just how long social psychology is going to be content, now that its radical, heroic stand against behaviorism has become part of mainstream psychology? It is something to wonder about. Some people are already talking rebellion from within, calling social cognition the "new imperialism." Listen to this call to the barricades from Robert Zajonc, himself one of the original founders of the social cognition movement:

> Social psychology is stagnant. It's right now borrowing concepts from cognitive science whose promise is uncertain. Straight cognition has done nothing but remain in people's heads. . . . A gang in Los Angeles choosing to take some chains and guns and go in the street shooting up some others is not going to be

> understood by the analysis of encoding, storage, and retrieval processes! This emphasis on social cognition has gone too far.

Social cognition will no doubt remain a major theme of social psychology for a long time to come—it has been too fruitful, and promises much more to come. But it would be no surprise if social psychology were about to undergo yet another momentous change. If so, who knows what it might be? But whatever the direction taken, we'd be surprised if it did not include what this chapter has described as a persistent preference of social psychology to study how people *experience* their world, regardless of so-called objective reality.

5

"Hey, You Guys on the Trapeze, Can I Ask You a Few Questions?"

Social Psychologists Love Doing Research

JOHN Arrowood is a University of Toronto social psychologist who studies social comparison processes. He was a student of Harold Kelley and Stanley Schachter during the exciting period when they were both at the University of Minnesota. But to us, Arrowood's chief claim to fame will always be the playful pleasure he took in being my dissertation adviser when, rather than showing an interest in his research, I took on what was by 1970 standards an outlandishly ridiculous dissertation project—an experimental study of love.[1]

Arrowood is tall, lean, bearded, charming, and a wonderful storyteller.[2] His eyes sparkle when he gets into a good one. I could just see the gleam in his eye when I asked him on the telephone why he had entered the field. His reply:

---

[1]Throughout this chapter, the first person refers to Art Aron.

[2]Actually, I was told to expect a fat "Jolly John" Arrowood but walked into his office my first day at Toronto and found a very slim man with a refrigerator full of diet soft drinks at his elbow. He has never gained back all the weight he lost in the late sixties. That's self-control.

> I had an undergraduate research scholarship for a summer and got to meet a number of . . . social psychologists who all seemed to be having the time of their lives doing things that you probably couldn't have stopped them from doing anyway. They were professionally nosy; they were curious. They were finding out new things—and they were getting *paid* for doing it!
>
> This came as a great revelation to me. . . . And so I was hooked at that point on research. There was simply no thought thereafter of going into law school.

Ellen Berscheid, a recent recipient of the Donald Campbell Award for Distinguished Research in Social Psychology, tells another story of being seduced by research. She was majoring in literature at the University of Nevada when she took a psychlogy course. She did not enjoy the course, but she impressed her professor, Paul Secord, who asked her to help on a research project. She loved the work, and when she was told she would have to become a psychology major to continue it, she reluctantly did so.

Later she married and moved to Minnesota, where she took a job with Pillsbury, doing research. She was promoted further than any previous woman, but the prejudice was still too much and she quit to take a job as a research assistant to Elliot Aronson (a consummate researcher whom you'll get to know later). Again she was told she could not do research unless she was a graduate student in psychology. And so she signed on, took the courses "the other kids in the lab were taking," "took the exams they took," and "before I knew it I had my doctorate." All for the love of research.

Perhaps Jerry Singer sums up these feelings about research best:

> It's just a satisfying feeling . . . when I'm doing it, things feel right . . . Getting the idea, going in and operationalizing it in the lab . . . piloting until it works, getting the study started and saying, "Hey, it's off the ground, it's going!"

It is our impression that social psychologists enjoy most of their work—research, theorizing, writing, presenting papers, teaching, consulting, discussing their work with colleagues and the public, and all the rest. But their favorite part is almost invariably the actual research. In this chapter we are going to break that activity down into parts: reviewing the literature, planning the research, carrying it out, analyzing the data, and writing up the study. In each case we will let social psychologists describe how they feel about it. Then we will give you one example from start to finish of what goes on inside a social psychologist's head while doing research.

A Look at Each of the Parts

Getting the idea is the first stage. But that has to do with theory, another area of social psychology pleasure, which we will consider in detail in the next chapter. Once an idea is in the wings, the show begins.

Reviewing the Literature

It may sound tedious, reading everything related to the topic you want to research, but it is exciting, too, as well as necessary.[3] You never know where your search will lead you, especially once you have become an expert in some specialized topic no one else knows as well as you. For example, Morton Deutsch's first assignment as Lewin's graduate student was to reveiw the literature on prejudice and intergroup relations. His next assignment was immediately to use what he had learned, by serving as a consultant to a Detroit school system!

One of our interviewees, Anthony Greenwald (a social psychologist at the University of Washington), provides a good sense of the delights to be found in reviewing the literature on a topic:

> There are few things that are more satisfying than discovering that something you are now reading fills in a gap or allows you

[3]However, when we asked Stanley Schachter about this stage, he told us, "Those of us in the Group Dynamics group were there at the start." Since there was no literature to review, "we never got in the habit." But that's Stanley Schachter. Besides, in his published papers, his reviews of the literature show the same thorough attention—and ill-concealed delight—that's true of all the other details of his research.

> to see how things can be combined in a way that you couldn't see before. The strongest example was when I discovered William James's treatment of idiomotor action, which helped produce a *Psychological Reveiw* article on idiomotor theory. So I discovered something in that case that had been written in 1890.

Or, as Zajonc put it, "Reading and learning in areas I know nothing about bring me surprise, excitement, growth—it's like going to a new restaurant and tasting something I've never tasted before. Discovery."

And reviewing the literature can bring even more surprises: Harold Kelley's entire career was changed by working with John Thibaut on a review of the literature on group problem-solving and process for a chapter for the *Handbook of Social Psychology* (1954). Kelley rememberred the job as being fun: "Seeing frameworks, seeing order, seeing that the field does cumulate. It does build up brick by brick by brick. . . . I enjoy that." But "the most exciting part was two minds digging stuff out and clicking." Although the two men had known each other since their days as students of Kurt Lewin, this was the first time they recognized their potential as a team. As a result of this project, Kelley discovered a congenial collaborator in John Thibaut. They went on to write much more together and to create their famous and fruitful *exchange theory* (1959, 1978). All in all, Kelley says this review of the literature "was the beginning of the most important intellectual development of my career."

In other words, when some social psychologist casually slips out the door saying, "I think I'll go on over to the library and review the literature for a little while," you never know what is going to come of it.

Planning the Research

This next step may be the most exciting of all: going from the idea, in light of a thorough knowledge of what's been done before in the area, to designing the actual procedures.

Elliot Aronson is a recognized master of the laboratory social psychology experiment. Lee Ross said that when planning an experiment, "I'd rather have ten minutes with Elliot than an hour with anyone else." And Aronson tends to talk about another famous researcher, his teacher Leon Festinger, when he describes the planning process:

> Festinger always said good ideas are a dime a dozen. The important thing is to take that idea and translate it into a set of experimental operations. . . . It's absolutely true. I see it as a very creative process. You get stimulated by an idea. Then the skill has to come. The real excitement is . . . constructing it so you can put it away for six months and go back to it and say, "that's about the only way that could have been done."
>
> There's a wonderful scene in [the film] *Amadeus,* when Mozart writes an opera and the emperor comes in and says, "Too many notes." Mozart says, "It couldn't have been done any differently." And I think that's the way I feel about certain experiments. They couldn't have been done any differently.
>
> . . . The casting of the scenario—I think that it must be the same kind of thrill that a novelist gets, or a playwright. And yet it's more interesting to me because it's in the interest of science, it's in the interest of truth.
>
> . . . You work it out and work it out and work it out, and what you come up with is a wonderful tapestry. And the critic comes along and says, "Ah, but that little thread in the tapestry is wrong and if you only could have replaced it with this." And then you realize that if you pull that thread, the whole thing is going to unravel. You can't just change one thing. You have to say, "If you don't like that scenario, you try one."

Aronson likens the work of the researcher to that of a dramatist; a social psychology experiment is a special re-creation of ordinary life. At its best it reveals that life to us. Or, as Lee Ross (whom you will recall from his fundamental attribution error quiz-show experiment) put it, an experiment can be thought of as a demonstration: "It's not so much a way of testing an idea, but a way of communicating an idea. It's producing a metaphor, or maybe an anecdote, or a vignette that allows you to communicate a point."

We have seen this element of drama and teaching in many of the studies described in previous chapters—from Lewin's study of leadership in boys' groups to Sherif's Robber's Cave studies, from Milgram's obedience and Asch's conformity studies to Schachter and Singer's experiments on the social determinants of emotion. But perhaps the ultimate demonstration was done by Philip Zimbardo.

Phil Zimbardo is one of social psychology's superb showmen, as well as one of its foremost contributers. When we asked him what he loves about planning research, he said:

> Just being aware of endless options at every point. . . . How you word things. How you present and how you arrange the laboratory. Each decision is challenging and can mean that a good idea will seem to be shown not to work, just because you've decided wrong. . . . It's risk taking.

We also asked him about the relationship between social psychology research and drama. He responded:

> What I do is straight theater. In fact, I co-teach a course now in psychology and drama. In many of my studies I have a script, a prepared scenario. There is scenery . . . there're actors. The only thing that's left to vary is the subject's response. That's the only improvisational part. Everything else is totally scripted. . . . And if you have it all down right and you have a good theory, then the audience applauds at the end exactly the way they're supposed to. And if your theory is not good, or the acting is not good, or the staging is not good, then it misses.

Now for our promised ultimate example of planning a dramatic study. Zimbardo, along with Craig Haney and Curtis Banks (Haney, Banks, & Zimbardo, 1973), was interested in the topic of deindividuation—the way a dehumanizing environment can totally change people in predictable ways despite their individual personalities. For this reason, these three researchers—along with some of their undergraduate students in an applied psychology course—were also interested in prisons and in the fact that deplorable prison conditions are not being changed even though in their present state prisons are known to be costly and ineffective. Haney, Banks, and Zimbardo suspected that this situation is due at least in part to people believing prisons are inevitably bad places since bad people fill them. The researchers thus set out to demonstrate that when placed in a genuine prison environment, completely normal people will quickly develop the same dehumanizing social environment seen in all prisons. In other words, when the scene on stage is a prison, the stage comes to control the actors, not the actors the stage.

Now here comes the wonderful planning. After their students tried a pilot study in the basement of a dorm, these researchers set out to create "a genuine prison environment" that was still legal, safe for subjects, and under their control. The researchers walled off a part of the basement of the psychology building at Stanford University. Three 6-by-9-foot cells were made, with steel-barred doors and no furniture except cots. A 2-by-2-by-7-foot unlit closet served as a potential solitary confinement. There was also a "yard" for exercise and guards' quarters were nearby.

Haney, Banks, and Zimbardo also decided to provide uniforms in order to increase anonymity: Guards would wear khakis, a whistle, a nightstick, and reflective sunglasses; the prisoners would wear loose-fitting muslin smocks, without underwear, and with an ID number on front and back, plus a chain and lock around one ankle, rubber sandals, and a nylon-stocking cap. No personal belongings would be allowed.

They decided to recruit subjects with an advertisement asking for male college students to be in a "study of prison life" and offering fifteen dollars a day for two weeks. Seventy-five students applied. The "most normal" twenty-two were selected after extensive interviewing. These subjects were randomly assigned to be guards or prisoners.

Guards were told they would serve eight-hour shfits. Their purpose was to maintain order, but they could not use physical force. Prisoners were to be given three supervised toilet visits and two hours of reading or letter writing a day, daily work assignments, two visiting periods per week, plus movie rights and exercise periods.

The students who would be prisoners were told to be available at their home or dormitory one Sunday night. The researchers arranged to have the students "arrested" by the Palo Alto City Police. They were charged, advised of their legal rights, handcuffed, carried to the police station in the rear of a squad car, booked, fingerprinted, questioned enough to prepare an ID file, and then placed in a detention cell. Next they were blindfolded and driven to the mock prison, where they were stripped, sprayed with a delousing solution, and made to stand alone, naked, in the cell yard, until given uniforms, photographed, and led to a cell. They were greeted and told the rules, to be memorized, and were thereafter told they would be referred to only by the numbers on their uniforms.

The researchers (now "wardens") had told the prisoners and guards that they were "free" to do whatever they wanted in their roles, as long as they followed the minimal "regulations." But in fact, as a result of all this careful planning of scene and set, this stage produced very decided role-taking. The guards became more and more abusive with their power as the prisoners became more and more passive. Privileges were never granted, and mere eating, sleeping, and eliminating became rewards rather than rights, rewards that were frequently denied. The level of psychological cruelty was quite extreme. The guards harassed, threatened, and insulted the prisoners, who did little to defend themselves. One went on a hunger strike, but the other prisoners, at the guards' encouragement, turned on him rather than joining him. Guards were always on time for their shifts and frequently stayed after. When the study finally was stopped, after only six days, the guards were actually disappointed. But the prisoners were so delighted that all but one was willing to quit even without being paid. Actually, five had already "quit"—with extreme reactions of depression, crying, rage, anxiety, and physical symptoms that required removing them early from the simulation.

The postexperiment period required equal planning, especially once the experimenters saw the extent of the involvement of these quite-normal students. All the participants met with the experimenters on several occasions over a year's time to talk about the experience, learn from it, and be certain there were no lasting effects. (Zimbardo thinks they were, in the end, better off for the experience.) All the subjects, and also the experimenters, were surprised by how potent the simulation had been. While it was probably painful for the Stanford researchers to see that they had caused so much suffering and sadism in normal people, it certainly must have been gratifying to see their careful planning result in such strong effects and, more important, to demonstrate a point they hope will save a great deal of suffering in the long run.

Carrying out the Research

This step of the research process—actually carrying out the study—varies a lot, and that may be the best part of it. One may be conducting surveys, directing a scene, introducing strangers—anything at all. While researchers do not always do this step themselves, they are always close by and eagerly involved. Anything can happen, and that is also part of the fun.

We asked Zimbardo how he felt about actually carrying out research, or what is called "running subjects" in an experiment (the phrase may have slipped in from behaviorists, who run rats through mazes):

> It's all discovery. Discovering individual differences, idiosyncratic reactions, seeing the phenomenon work firsthand. Because without it, all you have is numbers. You may as well have a pigeon in a Skinner box pressing a lever and generating numbers. What you anticipated with your formal . . . measures, that may not be all there is. If you don't actually run the subjects or observe them being run, you're not as likely to think about other questions to ask.

Judith Schwartz, commenting on her enjoyment of running "zillions of subjects" as a graduate student, harks back to the refrain of research as theater when she thinks about actually carrying out her experiments: "It felt like I was putting on a little play. I really liked that performing aspect."

Others told us they enjoy the observation of real social interactions or the sense of being on the spot, and in the spotlight, at a moment that may have historical significance for their field. But however they put it, for many social psychologists carrying out research is definitely one of life's pleasures.

Analyzing the Data

If you are not fond of statistics and computers, analyzing data can sound forbidding. But it is actually the most exciting, creative part of the research process for most of the social psychologists we interviewed. As Bill Graziano (of the University of Georgia) put it, "It's great fun, just great fun. . . . [It's like] trying to carve nature at its joints and you don't know where the joints are." Harry Reis called it "by far the most rewarding part." Deborah Richardson confided that this stage often puts her into "periods of euphoria." And Bibb Latane explained, "It's the stage where you need to use everything you've got—experience, intuition. . . . It's the moment of truth."

Which means that there can be frustrations too. In Russ Fazio's words, "I've certainly walked away from the office at the end of the day feeling very good, just very high about everything because data have come in as I expected. Or walked away feeling incredibly puzzled. Even depressed."

But win or lose, there's that excitement of first looking into the data and then analyzing and analyzing, looking for the jackpot. For just as there is a bit of the theatrical in social psychologists, there is a bit of the gambler too. Playing with the data is fun, and finding something really new is the big bonus—all the more so since this kind of winning adds knowledge to the world.

Winning is also how social psychologists as well as gamblers become sold on their respective professions. Recalling the very first study she ever conducted as a graduate student, Susan Fiske told us that "it seemed amazing to me that you could have a hypothesis and set up an experiment, and by golly, people would do what you said they were going to do. That seemed like great fun to me. I was hooked!"

Writing It Up

The final phase of research is letting people know about it, usually by writing a research article to be submitted to one of the journals in the field.

Not all social psychologists like writing as much as other aspects of the research process; some even find it a struggle.

But most of those we know enjoy it, and some find it the best part of all. Daryl Bem (whom you'll get to know in the next chapter) commented that he actually sees himself primarily as a writer: "I don't think I could ever make it doing fiction, so I do the next best thing. . . . I'm a writer who speaks in the language of data."

George McCall, at the University of Missouri at St. Louis, is most widely known for his elegant theorizing on the nature of identity. So far in his career, he has written nine books, including *Identities and Interaction* (coauthored with J. L. Simmons), which has become one of the most important books in sociological social psychology. Like Bem, McCall sees writing as central to his experience of social psychology:

> A lot of us are aspiring writers. There's something very rewarding about just doing things with words. Word play. The satisfactions of a good sentence that really said it, after eight cuts at it.

Similarly, Carl Backman, known for his theory of interpersonal congruency , says of writing that is is the most rewarding part of his work. "It allows me to make sense of what's going on.. . . Suddenly you can see how it can all be knitted together."

Of course, writing reaches its fulfillment only when that writing is in print so that it can communicate with others. To be certain that a particular article deserves publication, the journal to which it has been submitted will put it through a review process—two or three of the author's peers reading and commenting on the work. The article may be accepted as is, if all the reviewers are satisfied with it. But quite often they find some flaws, in which case the editor recommends "publish with revisions." Then the author receives the comments of the two or three reviewers and takes their advice into consideration. The third possibility is that the poor author will receive a rejection, with reasons, usually suggesting how further research might strengthen the article for submission to a different publication.

George McCall, whom we just mentioned, is also currently the editor of *Sociology Quarterly*. He was quick to praise the value of the review process: "It's like a triangulation in on what's the strength and what're the weaknesses of this particular piece of work."

Social psychologists also convey the results of their work in other ways, such as presentations at scientific meetings. But whatever way they do it, the joy, as Deborah Richardson notes, is in "sharing with other people what's come out of the work that I've done."

The Science and the Art

So that's the process: Review, plan, do, analyze, and write up. But we've tried to show that in social psychology, at least, this process is not cut-and-dried and that's that. It leaves a lot of room for fun, drama, risk taking, and creativity. Jerry Singer makes the point very well when he describes how he felt about learning behaviorist research methods while he was in graduate school and the contrast between that and social psychology research:

> You may get a twist in the terms of how you did the cards for the rat in a transposition—maybe dark gray on top and light gray on the bottom—but the methods were theme and variation of standardized methods. . . . The social psychology we were doing seemed to be much more rambling and free. It was sort of the difference between a very strict technical actor who has a script and then goes through a set of stock (although very difficult) techniques in order to present the material [and] a stand-up comic who's improvising while he is creating in front of an audience.

There are plenty of work and hard-core science to doing social psychology research. Even the stand-up comic comes off stage sweating, and even the social psychologist must be precise and rigorous at every step. But it really does seem that social psychologists, as John Arrowood said, get paid for what they love to do. Like artists and comedians, they would probably be willing to starve in order to express their creativity. But so far, they are paid enough to eat!

Moreover, like artists, actors, and gamblers, social psychologists keep at their work because someday they may make the Big Time—do a piece of research that truly changes the way people understand social life. Phil Shaver recalls that one of the greatest impacts on him as a graduate student was hearing his professor, Robert Zajonc, talking about research being an "art form" in which the "primary issue was creativity." Above all, Shaver recalls Zajonc saying that "the value of what you are doing is not really detectable at the time you are doing it. Many people are painting, and we don't know yet who is Picasso." That thought has sustained many a creative mind, whether that mind belongs to an artist, a scientist, or someone who is something of both.

In the next section our goal is to give you a description of one research effort in its entirety—an effort of our own, so we know it intimately.

Studying Love, Step by Step

I suppose getting the idea was the most enjoyable part. My research on love began when Elaine and I fell in love. It was while I was in graduate school at Berkeley. We met in a T-group (naturally) that was part of a class in small-group process taught by Hugh Coffey, who had studied under Lewin.

Since love was so much on my mind, I decided to study it, and by the time I was ready to do my dissertation, at the University of Toronto, I had already tried out several approaches. In one study I had people who were walking around with distorted glasses (in someone else's perception experiment) also rate their attraction to the person leading them around. This was to be a test of the effects of dependence. Not much came of that try.

I obviously needed more theoretical knowledge, to balance my personal, "practical experience." And so for my dissertation, and out of my own desire to be better prepared to research this area, I set out to "review the literature." That meant a summer in Berkeley ransacking the University of California library for every serious book ever written on the subject of love (there were very few in 1969), as well as locating the very few research studies that had been done up to that time.

I was quite moved by reading the clear insights on love that were twenty-five centuries old. I also gained a great deal from the more recent, systematic analyses of this century. But the real joy came when I would find a book or an article that clearly articulated something that had been my own intuition. I remember finding one obscure French monograph on passion that said exactly what I had been thinking and more. Then there was a study of attraction and aggression that used such ingenious methods that I later adapted them to suit my own purposes. Each of these discoveries would keep me coming back for more, like a rat to the lever in a Skinner box. Each discovery also kept Elaine and me up half the night, talking about our own love in light of these new thoughts.

Then came the fun of putting all the reading together into some semblance of order. It was a tremendously challenging, creative, and ultimately rewarding task. At the end, the wisdom of centuries, plus all sorts of other, tangentially related studies, all suddenly became an ordered understanding of something important to me. It was extremely satisfying.

By fall I had several clear ideas about what ought to generate love, or at least attraction, between people. All these ideas were based on the notion that there was more to falling in love than just the right combination of personalities (the main theory up until then). I and my obscure, passionate French-monograph writer (George Bataille) thought that what also mattered was the circumstances under which people met. In particular, people are more likely to be attracted to someone they meet during unusual, or "boundary breaking," experiences, such as those involving power, mystery, isolation, or strong emotions.

But how to create such boundary breaking experiences in the laboratory? I settled on the basic approach of having volunteer male subjects participate in a series of tasks with an attractive female student who they had been led to believe was another subject for the experiment but who was actually a student hired to play the part. This way, her attractiveness and personality would be a "constant" and any differences between groups of male subjects would be due to the different tasks or circumstances I set up. After doing the tasks together, the subjects would complete questionnaires in which a few questions, hidden among many others, would ask the real subject how attracted he was to "the other subject." Also, the male subjects would write a story to be analyzed for attraction by counting the number of romantic and sexual words in it (an idea I got from reviewing the previous research literature).

As for the situations, I tried several tasks. To "operationalize" mystery, I gave only partial descriptions of a person the subjects might meet and asked them how attracted they were to that person. The results were zilch.

But other ideas did work, and for the dissertation I settled on creating a strong emotional experience. It was "only simulated," like the Haney, Banks, Zimbardo prison study, but like that study, unexpectedly powerful in its effects. In the high-emotion condition, one of the scenes was that the subject played a captured soldier being tortured for information by the female subject. She would "torture" him by dripping "acid" (actually water) on him from an eyedropper until he would reveal his military secrets. I more or less directed, encouraging the subject to cry out whenever he felt the "acid" on his forehead, to try to feel as if it were actually excruciatingly painful, and to imagine that if it continued it would shortly burn through to his brain, killing him.

At the time, simulations were still a fairly new idea and I thought it would be hard to create emotion through role playing. I was wrong. The subjects' hands shook, they perspired, and when asked later, they all said yes, they felt *very* strong fear. As for my poor assistant, several times when we were done for the day, I had to help calm her down after she "had only pretended" to torture a half-dozen people.

In the control condition, she and the subjects played the same roles, except that the fluid really was supposed to be water, which she was using as part of a long, slow water torture and which at this early meeting the subject would not find very bothersome.

Of fifty-two subjects, only one guessed that the female student was actually our assistant. Our assistant never guessed that the extent to which the subjects were attracted to her was what was being measured. I was pleased with my directing, if surprised by its effectiveness.

With data in hand, I went to work on the statistical analysis. This was relatively simple—just a matter of plugging numbers into a computer and waiting for the result to come out. But at the emotional level, it was anything but simple. This was *my* Moment of Truth.

To my great delight, it worked. Those in the high-fear condition did show, for example, significantly more desire to kiss my confederate (one of the key questions) and wrote more romantic and sexual content into their stories. Looking at the details of these results, I found that the situation had generated, quite specifically, romantic attraction. Men in the high- and low-emotion situations showed no difference in their answers to the questions "How much would you like to have your partner in this experiment as a work partner?" and "How much would you like to have your partner in this experiment as a platonic friend?"

That study, together with the power study described in chapter I and my theoretical work, was my dissertation research (Aron, 1970). (Writing up my research and presenting it were an experience in itself, full of sleepless nights, camaraderie, and major and minor triumphs.) But these preliminary studies were just the first step. I wanted to know more about love and attraction, and I especially wanted to replicate these findings in a more realistic setting.

Fresh out of graduate school, I traveled west to Vancouver, where my friend and fellow social psychologist, Don Dutton, had just joined the faculty of the University of British Columbia. We were chatting one day, probably at Wreck Beach, about my findings and where to do the next study, when Don remembered just the place for arousing strong emotions—a scary suspension footbridge in a nearby provincial park. We went to see it.

This bridge was fear itself. It was about 400 feet of wobbly boards fastened to wire rope that swung in the breeze 100 feet above a raging river. (Later, just to be sure we were not the only cowards, we gave questionnaires to people who had just been on the bridge, asking them if they had felt anxious or tense out there. They had.)

Next there was the planning. Don, Elaine, and I talked for hours at our favorite Greek restaurant, thinking out all the details. We would have an attractive female student stand out at the middle of the bridge and stop each man walking over who looked between eighteen and forty and was alone. She would ask him to help her, right there and then, with a study she was doing for her sociology class on "creativity in beautiful places." If he agreed, she would hand him a clipboard and ask him to write a couple of brief stories based on pictures she would show him (essentially the same procedure used in the earlier laboratory experiments).

Then (we got really excited about this idea) when the man was done with the stories, she would tell him, "I'm sorry I can't tell you any more about the study until it is over. But it will be over tonight, and if you want you can phone me to learn more about it." She would tear off a piece of paper and write her first name and phone number on it. Our prediction, hunch, and hope were that those who were more attracted to her would be more likely to call.

This still left several problems. What would be the nonemotional control condition? We went back and found another bridge nearby, built of heavy cedar beams and crossing a shallow rivulet. Our female student could ask an equal number of men to fill out the questionnaire in the middle of this bridge.

Then there was the problem of the phone calls—who would actually receive the calls (not our poor, weary assistant)? And how would we know on which bridge the callers had met her? We solved this by having the assistant use a different first name for the two conditions—switching names on different days of the project. The names we chose were Donna and Gloria, because she would be carrying Don's briefcase, which was inscribed D.G.D.

Carrying out the study required one of us to drive our confederate to the bridge every day and stand by one end, unobtrusively watching to be sure everything went all right. About the only excitement to this part was the day the assistant came running to announce that a man was about to jump off the bridge. The park ranger and I talked him out of it.

Again, the statistics were simple. And again, the study worked. For example, of the twenty young men our assistant stopped on the scary bridge, eighteen telephoned that night. Of the twenty she stopped on the other bridge, only two phoned her. The results with the stories were also very clear.

Don and I wrote up the study, each taking parts of the article, and sent it off to a journal for publication. The editor liked the article, but he and two other reviewers said they had one reservation: Could it be that the attraction was due to the men seeing our assistant as a "lady in distress"?

That was something we hadn't thought of, and a very good point. So we tried it again, back at the laboratory this time. We decided to create the emotion by repeating that part of Schachter's affiliation study which told students they would be receiving strong electric shocks. We even used most of the Gregor Zillstein script, name and all. Some of the time the subject expected to get shocked and thought that the attractive female "subject" would also be shocked. Sometimes he was told that he would be shocked and not she, sometimes that she would be shocked and not he, and sometimes that neither would be shocked.

We reasoned that if the lady-in-distress theory were correct, the men would be more attracted to our assistant when they thought she would receive a shock, regardless of whether the man himself expected a shock. But if the idea of strong emotion, our original theory, were correct, the male subjects would be most attracted to the woman when the men themselves expected a shock, regardless of whether they thought she would be getting a shock or not.

An analysis of the data from this study found that the lady-in-distress theory, while a good idea, did not explain our results. But the strong emotion of the subjects completely explained them.

Now the article was accepted for publication (Dutton & Aron, 1974). And it has generated a good deal of exciting research since. Social psychologists especially seem to like it because it ties in with Schachter and Singer's results. Perhaps the subjects were experiencing an undifferentiated arousal caused by being on the scary bridge and thinking it was due to attraction to our assistant. This research effort has continued to be fun to discuss and tussle with for many years.[4]

In Conclusion: This Ticket Good for Any Ride

Social psychology research leaves so much room for freedom and has so many aspects that every social psychologist seems to passionately enjoy some part of it. Some glean the literature like Egyptologists putting together bits of papyrus from a tomb. Others like to put just the right question to nature, the one that will yield the unambiguous answer. Others like putting together the people, facilities, equipment, wording, and procedures, and refining the whole thing, until they have built a working drama that turns the researcher into a director, producer, writer, and perhaps supporting actor (the subject is always the star).

Then there are those who like actually carrying out the research, performance after performance, with all the camaraderie and excitement and good times that accompany any temporary, intense, meaningful endeavor. And some are addicted to that moment of truth—analyzing the results. Still others like broadcasting the results, sometimes literally, if the media get interested. Or putting it all together in a neal little package, working to get it published, and seeing it in print, one more addition to the total body of human knowledge.

---

[4]Foremost among the work following up on those studies have been experiments conducted by Greg White and his students (White, Fishbein, & Rutstein, 1981; White & Kight, 1984), in which they found greater attraction to the confederate following arousal due to such things as listening to a Steve Martin comedy tape, listening to a tape involving gruesome mutilations, or even just running in place for a few minutes. White recalls that he became interested in the topic after he had an experience of almost being in a plane crash and was very scared of flying. The next time he found himself having to board an airplane, he felt as if he

> was standing in line waiting to die. And I got tremendously attracted to some attractive-looking woman about my age. For forty-five or fifty minutes I was overwhelmed with this intense romantic attraction, and I kept wondering "What is going on?" I was actually debating—the plane is now in flight and we took off our seat belts—about trying to meet this person. Then all of a sudden I remembered the Dutton and Aron study. As soon as I did, the attraction went away, zilch, just like that.

But whatever part they like best, you can be sure they are enjoying it all. Because, for social psychologists, as Singer said, "Its just a satisfying feeling. When I'm doing it, things feel right."

6

"That's Just the Hypothesis. Wait till I Get to the Punchline."

Social Psychologists Are Intense Theory Builders

IN social psychology, good theory tends to be a personal, passionate endeavor. This is probably true for all good science, as we'll discuss in the last chapter. But as often seems to be the case, what is only a flavor in other fields tends to be a banquet in social psychology. The following example is at once a piece of history, a battle, and a drama. And it is also a prime example of theory building in social psychology.

The Leading Man

Leon Festinger was the prize theoretician among Kurt Lewin's students and uncontested King of Social Psychology for twenty years after Lewin died. His reign ended only when he became bored and abdicated, first taking up the study of perception, and now "the history of humankind." But as Festinger tells it, he would have been just as happy from the start as a professional chess player:

> I grew up in the Depression. It didn't seem one could survive on chess, and science is also a game. You have very strict ground

> rules in science and your ideas have to check out with the empirical world. That's very tough and also very fascinating. (Quoted in Cohen, 1977, p. 133)

So Festinger tried studying physics and then other sciences. But he turned to psychology, and eventually social psychology, because "The impression I was left with was that here was a field that was scientific and had questions to be answered" (quoted in Cohen, 1977, p. 132).

Festinger has always been a central and controversial figure. Even in Lewin's Quasselstrippe he was "the most exciting intellectually . . . the most stimulating" (from our interview with Morton Deutsch). Festinger was also usually the leader of whatever faction was fighting tooth and nail with other views, while Lewin looked on with a "benign smile" and always made it come out right in the end.

For the most part, you either loved Festinger or you hated him. Elliot Aronson, who was one of Festinger's many successful students, first tried to avoid him as a new graduate student at Stanford: "Festinger had a reputation for being terribly difficult and harsh with graduate students." Finally Aronson was shamed into attending a seminar of Festinger's, which because of Festinger's reputation almost nobody had signed up for. A friend of Aronson's asked him why he wasn't taking this seminar with this "very bright guy," and so Aronson agreed to attend. He was extremely impressed:

> It was the first time I ever saw a really brilliant research mind at work. Festinger had enormous confidence that he could do anything—look at the most interesting topics and examine them experimentally. That kind of intellectual flamboyance is remarkable and wonderful.

But it was also true, says Aronson, that Festinger

> was very impatient with sloppiness in thinking. He had a way of looking at you [if you slipped] that was a combination of impatience and sorrow—he really felt sorry for you because you were so dumb. . . . He didn't suffer fools gladly.

Festinger has always been notorious for irreverent remarks and behavior. After returning from a trip to the Orient, he reportedly commented that "the Wisdom of the East is errant nonsense" (though he did appreciate having learned to play the game of go, a kind of Japanese chess). Nor did he have the taste or talent for the kind of democratic leadership that Lewin had provided. Jerry Singer tells the following story:

> I was once on a committee which Leon chaired. We were planning a major conference and going back and forth about how to invite people when Leon said, "Tell you what, why don't we each suggest anybody we can think of who may even be topically appropriate? We'll put the names on the board, then we'll eliminate them until we've narrowed it down to those we think should be at the conference. . . ."
>
> Everybody concurred, names were suggested, and Leon stood up at the blackboard, writing them all down. Then when all the potential names had been exhausted, Leon said, "Okay, let's go through this. Number one. This person is not good because of" this, that, and the other thing. Zap. He scratches out the name with the chalk. "Number two. Here's a person that seems to be reasonable because his work's important and it fits this conference. I think we ought to keep this person for consideration." And he circles it. He goes through name after name, then comes to one that he says, "some people respect, but he's never done an experiment in his life and I think that this is totally inappropriate. . . ."
>
> But a very distinguished member of the committee interrupts and says, "Leon, I think we ought to consider this one further. He has a great following" and so on and so forth.
>
> Leon nods very sagely and says, "You know? You're absolutely right." And as he's saying this, his hand almost automatically is just scratching out the name entirely.

Singer emphasized to us that the point of this story is that Leon was usually two steps ahead of everyone else—ready to act while others were still processing information. Festinger *would* listen to criticism and change his ideas accordingly. But he could be caustic when he thought an argument was not well thought out. When asked about one famous critique of some of his work (a critique not altogether kind in tone), he immediately replied, "Yes—but that's garbage." When pressed, he proceeded to demolish it piece by piece.

Festinger earned the honored position he held. As Aronson recalls from his student years with him,

> He's a genius. And geniuses are very rare. He had the quickest, most courageous mind I'd ever seen in my life. And he didn't worry about failure. He could shrug off failure. And just went for it. Very, very smart. And very courageous. A rare combination. Along with the fact he was very well trained by Lewin.

Singer also praised Festinger's tremendous ability:

> He's able to think very directly about a problem without digression. He has a self-imposed intellectual rigor . . . he hits to the heart of the problem and he stays with it.

Then there are Robert Zajonc's Festinger stories, from when Zajonc was working with Harold Gerard at Michigan and Gerard was working with Festinger. Zajonc played "infinite ticktacktoe and darts" with Festinger and also sat in on some of the meetings between Festinger and Gerard. "Harold Gerard used to practice on me before he went to his meetings with Festinger—practice arguments, try them out. Then he would go into the meeting with Leon. . . . [Gerard] invariably lost the argument," recalls Zajonc.

But it was not just sheer brilliance that made Festinger remarkable. According to Phil Zimbardo, Festinger held his honored position because his personality was "charismatic." He "had the ability to attract bright people around him, and to inspire them with his brilliance."

Aronson describes another crucial aspect of Festinger's leadership that he remembers from his student years with him:

> Festinger, who I described as being tough, was also extraordinarily warm and sentimental. He could reminisce in a very warm, nostalgic way about Lewin—mostly about the goodness of the man, the brilliance of the man, and the atmosphere that existed around him.

Festinger created his own version of the Quasselstrippe. Aronson remembers a lot of camaraderie among the students and Festinger: "We used to meet once a week over at Leon's house in the evening, drink beer, and generate ideas together in a constant, consultative atmosphere."

Elaine Hatfield, another former student of Festinger's, has a similar impression from her student years:

> He was a lovely person to work for. He used to make people in the outside world angry all the time because he was irreverent. I think they just weren't used to someone from New York, with a sort of New York, Lower East Side fierceness. I think they took him seriously, when he just loved to say outrageous things. But he was always really kind to his students. He loved research. Yes, he was argumentative. I would train my students differently. . . . But I couldn't have had a better professor than Leon. I just loved to see him. . . . Students liked him so much that they all got together and tried to learn to play "My Yiddishe Mama" on mandolins and guitars because that was a song he liked a whole lot. . . . He did have all sorts of one-liners, sassy things he said to visitors. But he only picked on people his own size.

By 1957, Leon Festinger had already introduced several theories that are still among the most important in social psychology. But in that year his theory of cognitive dissonance was published (Festinger, 1957). Within one year it was the very center of American social psychology. And it stayed there for ten more years, because it was an exciting, simple, bold idea that explained a lot of human behavior. Even better, it did so in a way that seemed to fly in the face of common sense and of established thinking in the rest of psychology.

Festinger's cognitive dissonance theory says that people are uncomfortable when two beliefs they hold or a belief and something they have done are in conflict, or dissonant. To reduce this discomfort of dissonance, they are motivated to change either what they believe or what they do.

To demonstrate his point, Festinger did a study, with J. M. Carlsmith, a very bright undergraduate student of his at Stanford. This study is now so famous that it is known simply as

"Festinger and Carlsmith." In the study (Festinger & Carlsmith, 1959), male subjects first spent a half-hour placing and then removing twelve spools from a tray (they were told to do so "at your own speed") while the experimenter sat with a stopwatch, making copious notes on a pad. Then the tray was taken away and the subject spent the next half-hour with a board containing forty-eight square pegs that the subject turned, one at a time, a quarter turn clockwise, and then another quarter turn clockwise, and then another, and another.

After a subject had done these very boring tasks, the experimenter would explain that the experiment actually had two conditions: In the other condition, all the subjects were being told to do exactly the same tasks, except that first they were being told, by someone they thought was a previous subject, that the experiment was very enjoyable. This supposedly previous subject said things like "It was a lot of fun, I enjoyed myself; it was very interesting; it was intriguing; it was exciting." Having explained the "other condition" (which really didn't exist), the experimenter continued:

> Is that fairly clear how it is set up and what we're trying to do? . . . Now, I also have sort of a strange thing to ask you. The thing is this. [Long pause . . . with . . . a degree of embarrassment . . .] The fellow who normally does this for us couldn't do it today—he just phoned in, and something or other came up for him—so we've been looking around for someone that we could hire to do it for us. You see, we've got another subject waiting [looks at watch] who is supposed to be in that other condition. (Festinger and Carlsmith, 1959, p. 111)

At this point the subject would be offered money to play the part of the "previous subject" who found it all very interesting and exciting. Half were offered a dollar; half were offered twenty dollars. Only three of the fifty-one subjects who were asked to help out refused. And all but three more actually carried out their job of telling the "next subject," a young woman who was really a confederate of the experimenter, that it was an exciting task. In fact the situation was rigged so that she would say that someone she knew had taken the experiment and had said it was not at all interesting and she should try to get out of it. In order to carry out the job they had been asked to do, the true subjects then tended to say things like "Oh, no, it's really very interesting. I'm sure you'll enjoy it" (p. 206).

After all this, the true subject would be asked to complete some questionnaires about how interesting he had honestly found the experiment to be. Finally, the *real* experiment was explained.

The situation was intended to create dissonance between what the subjects initially knew from their experience (that the tasks were very boring) and their behavior (telling the woman it was interesting). Furthermore, Festinger and Carlsmith predicted, on the basis of dissonance theory, that the group paid twenty dollars would not suffer much dissonance, because they would simply explain to themselves that they had lied a little because they were being paid so handsomely to do so. (In 1959, twenty dollars was a *lot* of money for a ten-minute job.) But the group paid a dollar would suffer much more dissonance because they would have to ask themselves, in effect, "Why would I lie for only a dollar?" To resolve this conflict, they would decide that they had not lied that much, that the tasks were not actually so very dull. On the final questionnaire, the group paid a dollar were expected to show a greater liking for the experiment than the group paid twenty dollars.

The results were beautiful. There was almost no difference in the ratings of how enjoyable the tasks were between the group paid twenty dollars and another control group that had just done the tasks without being asked to do anything special afterward except complete the questionnaires. But the group paid one dollar rated the task as substantially more enjoyable.[1]

This result and the prediction on which it was based were revolutionary. So were the predictions and results of many dozens of other studies that came quickly on its heels. Elliot Aronson, who was Festinger's student, was one of dissonance theory's early champions. About dissonance theory's predictions, Aronson told us:

[1]The students were also asked to return the money afterward. Elliot Aronson, who was there at the time, remembers asking Carlsmith (who was personally conducting the experiment) about halfway through the study whether anyone had objected to returning the money. Only one subject had done so, someone in the one-dollar condition!

> As a community we have yet to recover from the impact of this research—fortunately! You see, for many working social psychologists, these results generated a great deal of enthusiasm and excitement, but for others, skepticism and anger. Because the finding departed from the general orientation accepted either tacitly or explicitly by most social psychologists in the 1950s: (that) high reward—never *low* reward—is accompanied by greater learning, greater conformity, greater performance, greater satisfaction, greater persuasion. . . . [But in Festinger and Carlsmith,] either reward theory made no prediction at all or the opposite prediction. These results represented a striking and convincing act of liberation from the dominance of a general reward-reinforcement theory.

Another radical aspect of the theory was that it forced psychologists in general to take mental events into account, something we said in chapter 4 was not at all acceptable at that time. Maybe *social* psychologists could be tolerated when they talked about thoughts or perceptions—but only as long as they stayed in their own domain. To challenge the rest of psychology with a theory that might refute both reward theory and behaviorism was sheer impudence. As Tony Greenwald, who has written extensively about dissonance theory (for example, Greenwald & Ronis, 1978), commented to us,

> Now we understand that the truth is almost the reverse of those generalizations [provided by behaviorism]. The smallest incentive you can possibly use to get someone to do something is likely to be the most effective in getting the person to like the activity and keep on doing it. The theoretical reason for this is that in the adult human, particularly, reward does not operate by instrumental learning and classical conditioning mechanisms, but by cognitive dissonance or attribution mechanisms, whereby people arrive at explanations for their own behavior by taking note of the conditions under which they generate the behavior. So this is a cognitive understanding of the way incentives operate rather than a mechanistic conditioning law.

Festinger suggested another reason the theory was unpopular: "The image of Man that was portrayed was not very idealistic . . . dissonance theory certainly contains the idea that people are willing to delude themselves and to twist the facts" (quoted in Cohen, 1977, p. 139).

Whatever the reason, some psychologists were angry. For example, at a Yale colloquium an eminent social psychologist pointedly and conspicuously fell asleep while Festinger was speaking. And a Yale student remembers that the first thing he was asked to do as a graduate student was run a study intended to prove Festinger wrong.

Others (including some at Yale) felt that this theory, along with Schachter's work on anxiety and affiliation, had "put social psychology on the map." As Aronson said, "The theory was fertile as hell. All we had to do was sit around and we could generate ten good hypotheses in an evening . . . the kinds of hypotheses that no one would have even dreamed of a few years earlier."

For example, one counterintuitive prediction, verified in a study by Aronson (Aronson & Mills, 1959), was that people who underwent a difficult, embarrassing "initiation" into a group would be more attracted to the group than those who had endured a less painful initiation. Another verified prediction (Aronson & Carlsmith, 1963) was that children who did not play with an originally very attractive and forbidden toy, but under conditions where violation of the prohibition would have resulted in only a very mild punishment, would find the toy less attractive than if there had been a large punishment for violating the prohibition. (According to the dissonance theorists, the children in the low-threatened-punishment condition, in order to reduce the dissonance of not playing with the desired toy, decided "I must really not like that toy very much after all.")

Yet another counterintuitive prediction of dissonance theory demonstrated by other researchers (for example, Ehrlich, Guttman, Schonback, & Mills, 1957) was that after making a decision (for example, to buy a particular brand of new car) people will then act in a number of subtle ways to justify that decision to themselves (for example, spend more time reading advertisements for the car they bought). The logic is that because they had been considering several options before the decision but have now chosen only one, the choice they make is dissonant with the other options they had been considering, and so now they must reduce this "postdecision dissonance."

But as Aronson points out, predictions that are "nonsensical in one decade can become 'common sense' several years later—and even old hat and boring in a third decade" (1980, p. 15). By the late 1960s, social psychologists' love of the new and the nonobvious had many looking for an alternative to dissonance theory. A review of the literature at the time commented on the "imperialistic dissonance hordes" that had mellowed, stating that "the youthful brashness of dissonance theory is [being] replaced by well-fed middle age" (Sears & Abeles, 1969). It was time for a new revolution.

Enter the Magician

In 1960, after receiving his bachelor's degree from Reed College in Portland, Oregon, Daryl Bem arrived at the Massachusetts Institute of Technology to study physics with a Woodrow Wilson fellowship and a reputation for independence and brilliance. Graduate students at MIT must take a minor, and they were encouraged to take it at nearby Harvard, in some subject unrelated to physics. Recalls Bem: "Everyone else I knew in physics was taking their minor in math. So I decided to take mine in social psychology." Before long he was spending more time at Harvard than at MIT. He has been a social psychologist ever since.

Bem actually finished his doctorate at the University of Michigan, where he was officially a student of Ted Newcomb (see the Bennington College study described in chapter 2). At Michigan, Bem was an iconoclast and an isolate. He never had an office near the other social psychology students or faculty. And he remembers that among them "there was a great rapport and group feeling . . . and I was always relatively peripheral. I got along with everyone. But I was pretty much a loner." This isolation could not have been helped by the fact that while he deeply valued the personal friendship and support he received from Newcomb, he chose as his real mentor a Skinnerian named Harland Lane.

Bem is not quite the colorful character of legend that Festinger is. Nor has he ever enjoyed anything like the fame and leadership that Festinger achieved. But neither is he dull.

For starters, Bem is an accomplished magician. Don Dutton reports that one evening after a conference, several social psychologists were sitting together and Bem performed a number of card tricks. For his final act, Bem took a new deck, let everyone inspect it, and asked someone to pick a card and not show it to him. He then removed his coat and tie and shirt. On his T-shirt was printed the card the person had chosen!

But his most famous magic trick was making the dominance of dissonance theory disappear. One social psychologist, John Touhey, recounts the excitement of the graduate students at that time:

> When Daryl Bem took all those ideas he took from B.F. Skinner (very loosely), gave them a symbolic interactionist cast, and reinterpreted dissonance theory—this was the major model of an upheaval in my graduate school days.

The upheaval was Bem's doctoral dissertation, and so he was truly a young upstart attacking the "well-fed status quo." As a social psychologist interested in attitudes, Bem set out to see if he could use behaviorist Skinnerian principles to change attitudes. In what he calls the "brown bread study," he had residents at a home for retarded boys recite the statement "I like brown bread" and gave them a small reward. As a control, another group of residents just listened to a narrator saying "You like brown bread" and received the same total amount of reward, at the end.

The experiment "failed" from at least the obvious Skinnerian point of view—receiving or not receiving a reward right after hearing or saying the statements made no difference in attitude—but *both* groups showed a substantial increase in brown-bread consumption. This result led Bem to "toy with the idea that self-persuasion is really a variant of interpersonal persuasion." That is, maybe it doesn't matter who says the words, as long as they are heard. Maybe we don't make as much of a distinction between ourselves and others as has been thought.

At about the same time, Lane had told Bem that "Skinner and I usually take the position that every person is really two people: the person behaving and the observer of the behavior." This view gave Bem the idea of merely describing a dissonance situation to subjects, so that they could act as observer. Having described a situation, he would have the subject infer what the attitude of the person in the situation must be. Bem thought that people hearing a description of a dissonance situation but not actually experiencing the supposed conflict would predict an expected final attitude for the person described to them that was no different from the final attitude that was actually reported by those in the real experiment. In other words, living through the conflict was not necessary. The situations did not create a strong "motivation" to achieve some sort of "balance" or freedom from internal dissonance. Persons in both the real experiment and the observational version of it simply looked at the behavior they performed or had described to them and said, probably quite calmly, "If I said that, I must have liked the experiment" or "If I said that, it was because I was paid a lot of money."

When Bem told his idea to Lane, "He bet me a strawberry soda that it wouldn't work—and I won the bet."

In one such study, Bem (1967a) merely described the Festinger and Carlsmith study, *from the subject's point of view*, step by step. He did not describe both conditions to each subject but described only the condition he had randomly assigned them to imagine.

The size and direction of the difference in questionnaire answers for the one-dollar and twenty-dollar conditions in Bem's observational version were almost identical to those of the original experiment!

Here was a revolution. It wasn't recognized immediately. Bem admits that his dissertation was "virtually unreadable, it was so heavy with Skinnerian language." Even when he published his dissertation studies in the *Journal of Experimental Social Psychology* (Bem, 1965), they were still in the language of behaviorism and Skinner. But as he continued to write and speak about his idea, Bem found himself becoming increasingly cognitive.[2]

Bem believes that Harold Kelley's (1967) Nebraska Symposium paper on attribution, which included Bem's theory as an example, is what finally brought his work into the mainstream of social psychology. His own changing of his language must have helped a great deal as well. (It was one thing to attack social psychologists' favorite theory, but to attack their very language and their assumption of the need for taking into account internal processes was too much.) With some practical advice from Ted Newcomb on how to go about it, Bem wrote an article (1967a) for the very prestigious and widely read *Psychological Review.*

This time his ideas did get a reaction. In Bem's own words, he had "attacked what was then King of the Hill, and the response was immediate." While there were many people in the wings who disliked dissonance theory, they had by now largely abandoned the fight, and for the next several years Bem stood his ground essentially alone, and with great vim and vigor, against the combined onslaught of Festinger's students and admirers. (Festinger himself had long since lost interest in the whole thing and was off studying perception.)

The first attack came from Judson Mills, who had been a student with Elliot Aronson under Festinger. Mills (1967) immediately published a reply pointing out that his own psychology students could not predict the results of Festinger and Carlsmith (thereby providing a quickie failure-to-replicate). But Bem (1967b) wrote back that Mills's students could not duplicate the result because the study had been described to them from the experimenter's perspective, not from what Bem held to be the subject's perspective.

[2]Bem was surprised by his growing use of cognitive concepts. He even included a long footnote in a 1972 summary of his work "apologizing " for his references to "inferential processes." But he found the cognitive language necessary. He told us that while it is possible to translate his ideas completely into behavioral terms, it is like trying to multiply and divide with roman numerals. He also feels it is a strength of his theory that it "survived the transition from a totally Skinnerian perspective to what to me was almost anathema in graduate school, which was a Heiderian phenomenological approach."

But as that response was being dealt with, a more sustained attack was forming. Bem relished it: "A group at Yale and Duke were independently, without each other's knowledge, trying to prove that I was wrong. . . . I was the one that told them about the other group. . . . Then they merged and the paper [Jones, Linder, Kiesler, Zanna, & Brehm, 1968] was published with several authors."

He also recalls:

> When I visited Duke, Jack Brehm [another former Festinger student] said to me, "Well, our experiments are now complete" (this was before they were published) "and we have found it much easier to refute your position than we thought." And I, being still young and green behind the ears, trembled in my boots. I was scared to death.
>
> But then when they published it, I thought they had essentially made the same misreading that Judson Mills had made. So I sort of enjoyed the whole thing. I enjoyed making the rejoinders. Any my perception is that I won.

Bem learned to stay quite mellow about the whole thing:

> Many of them seemed much more intense about it than I was. I thought it was kind of fun—after my initial trembling that they were going to smash everything I said . . . I was relatively relaxed about it.

Even his original hero, Skinner, was proud of him. Bem says:

> Skinner loved it. Someone once asked Skinner in one of his lectures, "What about dissonance theory?" and B.F. Skinner said, "Well, Bem has proven dissonance theory to be wrong"—an interesting reading of it. That's what B.F. Skinner wanted to believe.

Peace at Last

When Bem says he feels he won, he quickly explains that this is only in the sense that his ideas became part of the dominant paradigm that eventually took over social psychology, that of attribution theory, while dissonance theory moved to the back seat. But as an understanding of certain phenomena, dissonance theory will probably always be with us. It works better than self-perception theory in some situations, and Bem is the first to admit it. There are also some points that self-perception theory cannot explain—for example, that physiological arousal occurs during some cases of dissonance.

These days, Bem and Aronson, once warriors on opposing sides, both seem to approve, more or less, of a resolution offered by Russ Fazio, Mark Zanna, and Joel Cooper (1977). It says that both theories are correct but apply in different domains: When there is a large amount of discrepancy, dissonance theory works; when there is a small amount, self-perception theory works.[3]

In addition, peace came because the two theories are now seen as highly similar in their effect. For example, Ned Jones, one of the founders of attribution theory, considers the number-one achievement of social psychology so far to be Festinger's cognitive dissonance theory—"absolutely." He then explains that both dissonance theory and self-perception theory were getting at the same idea, really: "that not only do attitudes and other cognitive structures affect our behavior in ways that we can measure and make predictions about, but also, our behavior affects our attitudes. And Festinger was certainly there first with the idea."

One reason for Bem's own receptivity these days to cognitive dissonance as an explanation for some phenomena is that he knows he himself has experienced it. He has letters he wrote to his parents from the times before and after he switched from physics to psychology in graduate school—a situation with a large discrepancy for Bem. He comments that "the letters after the switch certainly show postdecision dissonance reduction. And that's not just self-perception. That had strong motivational and emotional content to it. So if you ask me, do I believe in dissonance theory—yes, I certainly do."

---

[3]Interestingly, this dispute between a Lewinian-influenced and a Skinnerian-influenced theory was resolved with the help of a third tradition of social psychology, the social judgment theory of Muzafer Sherif (whom you will remember from the Robber's Cave studies). This theory explains very clearly just when a discrepancy is sufficiently large to require a dissonance explanation.

Perhaps the basic problem with dissonance theory for Bem was that he also experiences the self-perception phenomena he has described, and he experiences them in many situations that, before he came along, cognitive dissonance had been used to explain. Even other people who know Bem have commented on the fact that he seems to do things first, then observe what he's done and use that to understand what he feels—just the way he has described self-perception theory. When we brought up this issue with him, he said:

> My wife [Sandra Bem, an influential social psychologist in the area of sex roles] could not possibly have made up self-perception theory because at the end of the day she'll say something like, "I'm feeling kind of depressed, I wonder why," and then she'll review the day's events to find out why. I'm much more likely to say, "Gee, I wonder how I feel? Well, today this happened and that happened. I guess I'm a little depressed." And that's self-perception theory. I tend to have very little access to my internal states and feelings. I've gotten better—nothing like marriage to help you have some access to your internal states and feelings.

And to soften the vehemence of a theoretical stance. But undoubtedly, now that social psychology is so focused on attribution theory, some new revolutionary is gleefully preparing to demolish the self-satisfied, attribution-theory status quo.

We should explain, by the way, that this love of revolution, this love of combat over particular theories, is not due to an inherent stubbornness. It is really a love of the intellectual adventure of finding "alternative explanations," other ways of explaining things. And it arises from the very nature of social psychology. As Harry Reis puts it,

> I tell my students that social psychology is probably one of the hardest courses to do well because it seems so deceptively simple at first glance. You first have to deprogram yourself. It's easier to learn something like physics, because you are learning something entirely new. You are not replacing any old beliefs, old wives' tales, any stuff that has been drilled into your head since you were two years old.

Thus the quest for alternatives to the usual explanations is very important to social psychology—perhaps even its essence.

Certainly the essence of cognitive dissonance theory was that it was an alternative explanation to reward theory and behaviorism. And the essence of self-perception theory was that it was an alternative explanation to cognitive dissonance. An interesting situation.

The Joy of Theory—A Heritage

Again, although social psychologists do enjoy these battles, the joy is not so much the skirmishing, but the insights that are pulled out of the field's brightest minds by this spirit of competition. And if the insights come from cooperation instead, which they do just as often, that's fine with everyone too. The point of this history of the dissonance and self-perception revolutions is that those involved were *openly and passionately* interested in the questions.

Like so many of the characteristics we have discussed, this rampant enthusiasm was modeled for later social psychologists by Lewin. Reportedly he could get so excited about ideas that when he was driving he would scare people nearly to death because he would take his hands off the wheel repeatedly to emphasize his points. Similarly, Dorwin Cartwright (1978) remembers Lewin, just a few months before his death, showing up late one night at Cartwright's house, bursting with excitement about some new idea.

When you love ideas, you find them everywhere. A school of theory about tension systems came from one of the Quasselstrippe's many visits to a Vienna café. Everyone would order coffee, then cake, then an hour later more coffee, then later more cake—and the waiter always remembered everyone's bill. But Donald MacKinnon (famous for his work on creativity) remembers that one night, a half-hour after everyone had paid, Lewin called the waiter over and asked him to write everyone's check again.

The waiter was indignant. "I don't know any longer what you people ordered. You paid your bill." And Lewin was delighted. He had wanted to demonstrate that a tension system had built up in the waiter, maintaining his memory, until the bills were paid. Many laboratory studies came out of this theory, called the "Zeigarnik effect." It all was the result of a visit to a café, with Lewin's mind present and working full steam (reported in Marrow, 1969).

Others feel a calmer love for good theories, but it seems to be just as intense. For Hal Kelley,

> it's like the thrill people might have got in the olden days from putting together clocks—putting together these little parts, getting the mechanism running, and then seeing what it generates when it runs. That's really a lot of fun, and it's part of what we do with theories—we take some simple assumptions, and set up some simple rules for inter-locking them, we set that little system going, and the thrills are when it generates something you hadn't anticipated.

Still others have said the joy of developing theory is "tackling the tough problems" (Anthony Pratkanis, who helped reconceptualize the relationship between attitude and memory); "puzzle-solving" (Margaret Clark who, along with Judson Mills, developed a widely cited theory of "exchange" versus "communal" types of relationships); "working out the structure of ideas, the flow and the connections, . . . the coacting effects, so that if the structure is right it works, and if not, it sort of sits there and rattles" (George McCall, the sociological social psychologist we've mentioned who created a very influential theory of identity and social interaction); and "seeing the connections—very different things coming together" (Phil Shaver, who extended Bowlby's attachment theory to adult love relationships).

Then there's Robert Zajonc's analogy: "A beautiful theory is like a symphony: It has very few assumptions and is rich in derivations. . . . Like Beethoven's Fifth [which begins] with four notes, three of which are the same—and manage to build a fantastic structure."

To some, theory represents independence. Self-assertion. Freedom. We've already caught this feeling from Bem, the Isolate, remaking the "in group's" social psychology until they *had* to notice. This feeling is well expressed by O.J. Harvey, a former student of Muzafer Sherif's (Harvey was the camp director in the Robber's Cave study) and well known for his theory of cognitive complexity:

> Rarely does a new fact shake the world. It's generally a capacity to look at old facts in a new framework. . . . Freedom is the ability to generate an option and act upon it. The ability to generate a new premise. We're trained and socialized . . . even in logic . . . we're always given the premise in society by someone else, and we're punished if we take premises that are deviant from the extant ones. We're called infidels in religion, we're called traitors in society. . . . But big discoveries come from the ability to take some new premise, some new perspective.

Or as John Touhey (a social psychologist whose work is in the more sociological, symbolic interactionist tradition) remarked about social psychology,

> It hasn't crystallized or hardened or limited itself to any narrow approaches. What I find wonderful about doing social psychology is that I'm free to bring in ideas from all of the allied social sciences and from the humanities as well. That's the charm, that to me is the cream—the fascination, the addiction, if you will—of modern social psychology.

This freedom, this love of wild ideas,is actively taught to each generation of social psychologists. An example is Stanley Schachter, who emphasizes to his students that they shouldn't waste their time studying *bubbe* psychology. *Bubbe psychology* is the study of what's obvious—the kind of finding that when you tell your grandmother (the Yiddish *bubbe*), she says, "so what else is new? They pay you for this?"

Aronson clarifies the point: "That doesn't mean we never test a *bubbe* hypothesis. But if all your psychology is *bubbe*, what the hell's the sense of being in the business?" It's more fun to show that the more people available to help, the less likely any one of them will help (Latane & Darley, 1970). Or that the less you reward people to change, the more they change (Festinger & Carlsmith, 1959). Or that people can be made to say and even see the opposite of what is "obvious" to anyone (Asch, 1958).

Nor was Bem the last social psychologist to challenge the theoretical status quo. The field abounds with new and often highly revolutionary ideas that, at the least, shake things up enough to keep anyone from napping too long in "dogmatic slumbers."

We have had some experience rocking the boat ourselves, with several theories. In addition to our work on love (some of which was described in chapter 5), the biggest fun for us has come from a radical theory of social influence that arose from studies showing reductions in crime rates and other social changes associated with small numbers of people practicing Transcendental Meditation (see, for example, Dillbeck, Landrith, & Orme-Johnson, 1981). To verify that finding ourselves, experimentally, we moved groups of meditators in and out of high-crime areas of cities and found, to our astonishment, that the presence of people meditating together nightly in an area—just meditating, doing nothing else—yielded reliable reductions in the areas' crime rates. It was hard to believe but also very, very hard to ignore, especially after four more replications. We will never forget the experience of presenting these results to a roomful of fellow social psychologists at an American Psychological Association meeting (Aron & Aron, 1981).

A more recent case of going against the established way of looking at things is a theoretical proposal that, although having less extreme implications than the previous example, still earned its share of shaking heads when it was presented at a recent meeting of the Society for Experimental Social Psychology. Robert Zajonc (the social psychologist we described in chapter 1 as one of the field's most successful exemplars of chutzpah) thinks emotions may in part be explained by an obscure turn-of-the-century French theory (Wayenbaum, 1907) proposing that facial expressions affect the blood flow to the brain, and the changed blood flow is what is responsible for different emotional experiences (Zajonc, 1985).

What is most satisfying is that one social psychologist (who must remain anonymous because of the rules for reviewing grant proposals) recently reviewed a grant proposal from Zajonc for further funding of his research on his facial-blood-flow idea and said:

> I have to admit I thought it was slightly crazy and very different from what other people are doing. Yet I was very enthusiastic about funding it. If he was right, it was really important. It's much better to fund than something that's a tiny little step and is probably right and is not very exciting and not very important.

Even so, when working on a new theory, one that flies in the face of common sense and established wisdom, the researcher may feel like an outsider. The ability to withstand that isolation, even enjoy it, while pursuing a new idea may be the essence of and the secret of at least some of social psychology's successful theory builders. Yet, the social support that social psychologists give to one another is also part of that success. Rather than being threatened by an idea they do not fully grasp, as we saw in the case of the reviewer of Zajonc's grant proposal, they are unusually willing to understand and even likely to enjoy someone daring to try to turn psychology on its ears.

Elaine Hatfield suggested to us that this tradition of seeing beyond the common scene and status quo, of standing one's ground enthusiastically when challenging what is accepted, and of supporting others who do so may result from the fact that numerous social psychologists have been either members of ethnic or racial minority groups or immigrants. Stated Hatfield:

> They have a disadvantage in that they never have as much self-confidence as someone who has been in the majority group their whole life. But they have an advantage that far outweighs that—they see all sorts of things they are not supposed to see.

A number of social psychologists have commented on this tendency of social psychologists to come, as Deborah Richardson put it, "from not perfectly benefited backgrounds." Some of those we interviewed commented on this kind of experience in their own lives. Historically, there have been many Jewish and Italian social psychologists, especially. Muzafer Sherif was Turkish. And even those who wre "white Protestants" were sometimes minorities in their own ways: Craig Haney (of Stanford prison study fame) for example, was about the only white growing up in a black neighborhood.

In Conclusion: More Crazy Horses, Please

Social psychologists have criticized themselves for having too many chiefs and not enough Indians. And, of course, social psychology would not progress without those who develop smaller theories about particular issues and those who test, flesh out, and refine the big ones. But perhaps in a science tackling issues that are so close to daily experience and common sense, where there is always a risk of falling into the *bubbe*, social psychology can stand as many Crazy Horses and Geronimos as it can produce.

7

"We Have a Dream. Still."

Social Psychology Persistently Tackles Social Problems

MUZAFER Sherif told us how he got into social psychology, or "the study of human relations," as he prefers to call it. It was 1919 and the Greeks were arriving to occupy his native province in Turkey. Sherif was only fourteen or fifteen, but "I was always, even at that time, curious about seeing things for myself." So he went down to where the troops were disembarking:

> They came . . . and they started killing people right and left. The immediate thing that concerned me was that somebody else beside me was killed. . . . And I thought it was my friend and that I'd be killed too that day. Then the soldier . . . looked at me for a few minutes. He was ready to stab me. Then he walked away.
>
> That enmity that led people to kill each other made a great impression on me. There and then I became interested in understanding why these things were happening among human beings. I didn't know what profession I'd follow—the technical term for it—but I wanted to learn whatever science or specialization was needed to understand this intergroup savagery. I wanted to understand, and I devoted myself to studying human relations.

We have already seen how Hitler caused many social psychologists to direct their efforts toward understanding and preventing all that nazism had been able to do to a nation of normal people. Sherif's story is another verse in the same song. In fact, ask almost any social psychologist why he or she chose the profession, and he or she will tell you something like "I wanted to understand how people could be so cruel." Or so uncaring. Or so stupid. Or the person wanted to fight injustice, understand prejudice, help people get along with one another, prevent war. Or just help others live a happier, more loving, more fulfilling life. It is not true for every last one of them, but it seems to be true for most. It is as though a large number of social psychologists have appointed themselves to be our species' self-improvement committee.

Here is another good example. We remember David Krech as the distinguished elder statesman of psychology who walked the Berkeley campus in the late 1960s with his cane and an air of great dignity. One of us took history of psychology from him; the other learned social psychology from his textbook, a thoroughly but subtly idealistic treatment. His reputation was as a hero of the loyalty-oath struggle of the McCarthy era and as a sympathizer with the late sixties' student "revolution."

During the Great Depression, however, David Krech (1975) was Isodore Krechevsky and he was running rat experiments at the University of Chicago, his umpteenth temporary, part-time, poorly paid appointment. Although he had published and was well respected as a psychologist, he was a Jew, which meant that even in the United States his chances were nil of winning one of the few regular university positions open at all during the depression.

Until then, the studious Krechevsky had been largely oblivious to political and social events outside the laboratory walls. But by 1933 he could no longer ignore either his own mistreatment or the general state of joblessness and hopelessness in the world around him.

Krechevsky, in his spare time, became a political activist. In 1935 he and some friends in Chicago got the idea that their social concerns might be shared by many other young psychologists (and, it turned out, by many senior colleagues as well). They formed an organization of psychologists "for the promotion and protection of research on 'controversial' topics . . . the authoritative interpretation of the attitudes of the socially-minded psychologists respecting important group conflicts, and the support of all progressive action that promises to aid in the preservation or creation of human values" (quoted in Finison, 1979, p. 30). They called their organization the Society for the Psychological Study of Social Issues, known as SPSSI, affectionately pronounced "Spissey."

While SPSSI was and is open to all psychologists, it has long been dominated by social psychology. As soon as it was formed it was joined by every major social psychologist of the time—Murphy, Newcomb, Floyd and Gordon Allport, Sherif, and, of course, Lewin and all his gang. Today more than three thousand belong, mostly social psychologists. According to social psychologist Marilyn Brewer, a recent president,

> It's an institutional identity for certain positions. . . . And its a place to which people refer certain kinds of questions. Psychologists say, "That's a SPSSI issue, let's see what SPSSI people say." . . . I don't think of it primarily as a political activist organization. There are occasions when it has been. But mostly its purpose has been to give all forms of support—from money to credibility—to people who want to do work which has social relevance.

Throughout the years SPSSI has been many things to many people, but it has always been a refuge for the politically aware social psychologist. With each new wave of social concerns in the United States, new generations of social psychologists have created or joined organizations to deal with it. During the early 1950s, young social psychologists interested in peace (a dirty word in those McCarthy, red-baiting years) formed the "radical" Research Exchange. Social Psychologists for Social Action was formed during the Vietnam era. Both these organizations were eventually incorporated into SPSSI. In the past decade, new concerns, about women's rights, nuclear weapons, child abuse, and many other issues, have led to organizations of mainly social psychologists, new "committees" of SPSSI, or both.

SPSSI and its cousins are one outward manifestation of what we want to talk about in this chapter. The main point is that few social psychologists are ivory-tower academicians. They care about the world. They want to make a difference. The characteristic is almost universal among social psychologists.

Not that they agree on *how* to make the difference; that would be too much to ask. In particular, there is one main division among social psychologists, and we'll be discussing it: There are (a) those who think the pursuit of "pure science" will best serve "applied" purposes in the long run and (b) those who believe it is important to work directly on applied issues. To lead up to that question we must begin where we always seem to have to begin, with Lewin.

Action Research

Like Krech, Lewin started out just interested in psychology, pure and simple. But the events in his native Germany forced him to look around, and he gradually turned more toward social psychology.

He found racial and ethnic prejudice in the United States too, much as he loved the country and wanted not to see faults. Thus, by the early 1940s he had already conducted the famous study of authoritarian and democratic leadership and was saying that it was not enough for psychology to understand behavior: "We must be equally concerned with discovering how people can change their ways so that they learn to behave better" (quoted in Marrow, 1969, p. 158). By the end of the war, Lewin had become committed to his often-cited dictum that there should be "no action without research; no research without action" (quoted in Marrow, 1969, p. 193).

Indeed, by 1946 Lewin had set up not one but two institutes to create and apply knowledge. One of them was the Commission on Community Interrelations (CCI), which he had persuaded the American Jewish Congress to fund as an institute to study and reduce intergroup tensions and prejudice. For its motto, he suggested the two-thousand-year-old saying from the famous rabbi Hillel:

If I am not for myself, who will be for me?
If I am for myself alone, what am I?
And if not now, when?

At the same time, Lewin founded the Center for Group Dynamics at the Massachusetts Institute of Technology. The site was not accidental.[1] MIT focused on science and engineering—pure knowledge, along with its application. Likewise, his new enterprise would integrate theoretical and experimental social psychology with its applications, by creating "experiments in change":

> [This goal of integrating the two] can be accomplished . . . if the theorist does not look toward applied problems with highbrow aversion or with a fear of social problems, and if the applied psychologist realizes that there is nothing so practical as a good theory. (Lewin, 1951b, p. 169)

Chapter 3 described some of the work done or inspired by the Center for Group Dynamics. Now let us look at some of the very practical problems Lewin took on for his Commission on Community Interrelations. While the goal was always to unite theory with practice, in this case practice tended to pay the bills: The CCI's funding came from the American Jewish Congress, which needed Lewin to make news by solving some real disputes if the organization was going to be able to continue to rationalize giving money to CCI.

The first problem CCI took on was an incident between Jewish and Italian-Catholic teenage gangs, especially the latter's disturbance of Yom Kippur services at a synagogue in Coney Island. Lewin created a team to investigate, and it found that the attack was not so much against Jews as it was a venting of frustration due to lack of adequate housing, recreational facilities, and the like. Accordingly, Lewin simultaneously worked with the mayor's office to improve conditions and sent in a

[1]Accident apparently helped a little. Supposedly Lewin would not have minded locating in Berkeley, either, with its warm winters and congenial social and political climate. But the proposed center's letter of acceptance from the University of California came two days too late.

staff member, Russell Hogrefe, to work with the gang that had started the trouble. A year later the gang was behaving in much more socially acceptable ways, and CCI's methods of changing the gang's behavior was later adopted by other agencies all over the country.

CCI also took on the problem of quotas for Jews in the admissions policies of universities. Conferring with American Jewish Congress members, Lewin argued that forcing discriminatory policies to be changed would eventually lessen prejudice. This approach would be better in this case, he thought, than relying on decreased prejudice to lead eventually to better policies. As a result of his advice, the American Jewish Congress brought a suit against Columbia University's medical school and won. Lewin's point—that in the case of prejudice you can sometimes "legislate morality"—proved true years later, during and after the civil rights movement, and was no doubt behind the thinking of the Equal Rights Amendment. (It was also a point that later was to become the core of Festinger's cognitive dissonance theory.)

CCI also helped blacks get jobs at New York department stores. The stores argued that white customers would not buy from black sales personnel, but CCI did opinion surveys that demonstrated the argument was not true.

CCI disproved yet another myth, too—that Jews always voted for other Jews. That study was done by Festinger.

Perhaps the most influential study from this period was done by Morton Deutsch and Mary Evans Collins (1951), on integrated housing.

It was a simple study comparing housing projects in New York City with projects in Newark, its neighbor across the Hudson River. The housing projects were nearly identical, except that Newark's were segregated, with blacks in different buildings checkerboarded around the project, whereas New York's project buildings were thoroughly integrated. The question was, Did living in close proximity increase or decrease prejudice among the races?

Deutsch and Collins found that integration in these projects dramatically decreased prejudice. Those in the integrated buildings seemed to share a growing feeling of their common humanity. Hostility was being replaced by friendliness. Residents wanted to see their buildings even more integrated. In the segregated projects, whites were more prejudiced against blacks, wanted still greater segregation, and expressed more hostility, even toward other whites. It had always been assumed that whites at least had to outnumber blacks for the whites to accept integration. But in fact, the best race relations seemed to be in a project that was 70 percent black.

The study bore much fruit, most of it sweet. While one pro-segregation group used it for evidence that integration should be prevented because otherwise the races would become too friendly (!), most public officials saw the point. Deutsch told us that because of the research, the Newark Housing Authority, where they did the study,

> found themselves under pressure from a lot of citizens groups to desegregate, and with the research results and I think the basic willingness of the Authority, they in fact desegregated the housing project and no longer maintained separate buildings for blacks and whites.

In those postwar years everyone around Lewin felt the heady thrill of maybe being able to *do* something about social problems. From 1946 to 1950, fifty separate projects were carried out by CCI. Lewin's excitement about the whole thing was extreme even for him. It was a time of great creativity for him. In fact, some of Lewin's associates think his frenetic activity led to his early death in 1947. Not only was he still an active theorist and a social activist, but he was personally raising funds and maintaining public relations for his new institutes.

Gertrud Lewin, Kurt's wife, reminisced about this period:

> Kurt Lewin was so constantly and predominantly preoccupied with the task of advancing the conceptual representation of the social-psychological world, and at the same time he was so filled with the urgent desire to make use of his theoretical insight for building a better world, that it is difficult to decide which of these two sources of motivation flowed with greater energy or vigor. (G. Lewin, 1948, p. xv)

From a Strong Trunk, Two Healthy Branches

Kurt Lewin's ability to integrate applied and theoretical social psychology was a feat that, so far, no one else has managed with the same adroitness. Even among his students and associates it was not the same smooth melding. Deutsch recounts the meetings of the Quasselstrippe at MIT:

> Lewin had different attitudes toward different people. Lippitt represented the applied aspect that Lewin was interested in, while Festinger represented a bright, theoretical, experimental kind of person. . . . There was a clash of orientations. . . . Not inevitably, but in fact there was such a clash. Festinger represented "science" and Lippitt represented "practice."
>
> [Lewin] encouraged vigorous debate. And there was a good deal of that. But he personally represented the fusion of a variety of interests. . . . So he would be able to somehow bring the positive strands from the conflicting orientations and weave them together into some unified position. And there was a certain . . . charismatic quality . . . he could pull things together and somehow everyone would feel enlightened.
>
> I do think there was a split after Lewin died. There was a group that got symbolized by Lippitt and Bethel and T-groups. . . . And then there was a group that got symbolized by Festinger and which represented a harder, experimental, theory-oriented approach. For a while—ten or fifteen years—there was a kind of division in social psychology around that. But certainly in the last ten years, maybe even longer, that has no longer been true.

Other social psychologists we spoke with see this division as still not entirely healed. But everyone we spoke with, from those doing the most esoteric "pure" research on the thinking process to those conducting workshops on international peace, agreed that they want social psychology to have important practical value. The differences among social psychologists are mainly ones of strategy.

To Be Objectively Compassionate or Compassionately Objective

A number of social psychologists believe that the most important thing they can do to contribute to the betterment of humankind is to conduct the most purely theoretical, experimental research possible, so that they will discover principles that can be broadly applied. For example, Lee Ross emphasized:

> I think that the classic experiments that have contributed to theory development are more useful to the applied researcher than any particular applied study that has ever been done. . . . Part of it is that most applied research by its very nature has a degree of specificity about it that makes it not terrifically helpful in the way you think about the next situation. A classic theoretical study may be more relevant to the next thing you do than the last applied thing you do.
>
> If you want to understand why social change has been so much harder to accomplish than all the applied psychologists thought it would be, the answers are to be found in theoretical social psychology, not in probing through the notes of applied psychologists.

Russell Fazio, whose work on cognitive processes is very much theory-oriented research, comments:

> I've always viewed our field as one that was primarily concerned with basic research and the establishment of theories and models. But I don't have any doubt that if we continue to build this theoretical foundation, we'll be able to apply it if we want to.

What you are hearing is a caution. Traditionally, science is "pure." Physics doesn't worry about whether its discoveries will help space travel or the energy problem. Those problems are left to be solved by engineers and inventors—the people who apply science. Scientists fear that if they limit their thinking to what is needed at the moment, not only will they not make the type of basic discoveries that in the past have proved most fruitful in the long run, but they won't be as objective, being in someone's pay or focused on some one group's problem or out to prove a particular ideological point.

Alice Eagley, a major contributor to the social psychology of gender, spoke to us at length on this point, because her research is so relevant to women's issues. She said, "I find it is very hard to [present a finding to some people] that doesn't fit the liberal feminist ideology—which I share to a great extent." She sees being frequently misquoted and her data misinterpreted as "an interesting case history of science coming into confrontation with social action." But she has a faith that

> if we are good social scientists and tell the truth—use the scientific method—in the long run that is better for women. To suppress a finding and use some other that some kind of audience wants to hear—I think that's selling out as a scientist. It sells a false reality, and what we want for women, and others too, is to understand the reality as it is and to move in terms of that. We cannot build a social movement on shaky ground.

Still, the caution of people like Fazio and Eagley clearly overlies a continuous concern in social psychology for relevance, a concern for people. From many of the social psychologists we talked with, we could hear the constant struggle between the desire to help and the desire to be what they saw as the *most* help, by contributing solid knowledge and not wishful thinking.

As Anthony Pratkanis, a theoretically oriented social psychologist, says, "I am a Lewinian." Which to him means he not only expects his work to be applied but expects its application to rebound and improve his future theories. "But what worries me," he says, "are those who follow what I call a social welfare model, where they end up only researching one specific domain and never rise above that little domain to see the larger theoretical picture."

Dalmas Taylor, a black social psychologist at the University of Maryland, has his own resolution of this internal conflict—what we will call the "two hats solution." He says:

> The problem is that when you are involved in studying something, it requires a certain amount of objectivity and detachment. When you are involved in pursuing a remedy, there is less objectivity and a great deal of attachment. So you essentially end up wearing two hats, playing two different roles. I think that can be done, but it's very *difficult*. . . . What we have is a series of methodological strategies that mitigate our biases, and I think they perform a sufficient check and balance to let us play this dual role with less concern and less error. . . .

> I am a minority, so I come to this with a sensitivity of someone who is a member of an oppressed, disadvantaged, and excluded group. I have been keenly interested both personally and professionally in eliminating the factors in our society that perpetuate prejudice, racism, and discrimination of any kind. I'm just committed to trying to make a change in institutions and in people. I've been involved in social responsibility in investment and the advocacy of economic boycotts of South Africa, and so on. Some of this obviously goes beyond anything that our data inform us of, but that's the duality of being a professional who cares about these issues and being an individual who has a personal commitment to social change.

Still, what has been most personally satisfying for Taylor is not the application of his expertise to particular problems but "providing a conceptualization and explanation of the dynamics of prejudice and racism that in some ways challenge the status quo." Once again we hear about the love of theory and the value of theory, even for solving concrete problems.

Getting the Fruit off the Branch and into the People

The problem, of course, is that if most social psychologists stick to pure science, who is applying all these findings to the problems that they all agree they want solved? Chemical companies apply chemistry, oil companies apply geology, but who applies social psychology? Some ideas are used by advertising and opinion pollsters, but much of the findings would be best used, especially in the opinion of socially concerned social psychologists, in public agencies and institutions like government, schools, services for the disadvantaged, and rehabilitation settings—institutions that often lack the personnel to find out about or apply social science theory and findings to their problems.

For that matter, even the brightest practitioners and social policymakers tend not to know about social psychology findings, probably couldn't understand the jargon if they did read the research journals in which the findings are hidden, and certainly would have a hard time seeing any practical implications of "the fundamental attribution error" or "cognitive dissonance" for their own policy or problem area.

This question of how to see that social psychology knowledge is applied has been of particular interet to M. Brewster Smith, a student of Gordon Allport and a social psychologist who has had a long, illustrious career, including presiding over the American Psychological Association and SPSSI. One of Smith's greatest interests is the application of social psychology to the prevention of nuclear war and to political issues generally, and he is able to point to at least a few instances in which social psychology's ideas have reached top decision-makers. For example, Smith cites a speech by Jack Kennedy in 1963 in which JFK proposed a unilateral test ban treaty and invited the Soviets to take other unilateral initiatives; historical evidence suggests that this speech reflected the theories of social psychologist Charles Osgood on conflict reduction, as these theories were apparently well appreciated by those close to the president.

But Smith admits that right now

> there is not any great readiness of the inner circles to pay much attention to our ilk. Therefore our role in these times is more to arm those who are trying to educate the broader public. To present them with perspectives that have not been front and center, like the inherent nature of the conflict process, for example—White's and Bronfenbrenner's stuff on the way each side sees itself as defending, the other side threatening. [Our goal should be] to get those ideas into the social bloodstream.

But it's a frustrating task for a social psychologist. As Ned Jones put it, "I think we have a lot to say—at least as much to contribute as economics and political science." It is therefore not surprising that many social psychologists believe that if they want to see their work applied, they will have to apply it themselves. For example, Don Dutton (see chapter 5) is now studying the effect of misattribution of arousal on family violence. Elaine Hatfield, perhaps the foremost pioneer in research on love, has an active marital-therapy practice, wherein she directly applies the results of her own and others' research. John Gottman, whose research on marital communication you read about in chapter 3, has helped create marital-communication training programs based on his work. And O.J. Harvey, one of the researchers on the Robber's Cave study, has since worked on applying his theories of cognitive flexibility and belief systems to education.

Another approach to getting ideas applied is to make social psychology research so dramatic and obvious that the applications can't be missed. This was Sherif's strategy with the Robber's Cave studies of intergroup conflict and conflict resolution. And it was Phil Zimbardo's strategy with the Stanford prison study described in chapter 5; he used his very clear, relatively straightforward findings to try to persuade correctional authorities and other public officials to make changes in the prison system.

Last but not least is the approach of teaching. Social psychologists are, after all, usually professors. During their career they may teach many tens of thousands of students, the vast majority of whom will not become social psychologists but will be in a position to use social psychology personally or professionally. Teaching is obviously an important opportunity to point out the practical implications of theories.

The Well-Trained Mind Bears Fruit

We first suggested that there are two branches to this tree of strategies for expressing social concern: a pure science branch and an applied branch. But by now you can see that it might be more accurate to say there are many branches. Or better, a continuum of branches, bearing social psychologists of all types, from those not at all concerned as professionals with any practical implications of social psychology; to those who are concerned but feel pure research and theory serve humankind best in the long run; to those who are also concerned and agree that pure science serves best *but* make an extra, personal effort to get the pure science applied (we just finished describing that branch).

But there is one more limb to the tree, the branch of direct, applied, or "action research." Applied research uses the theories and especially the methods of social psychology to study and solve specific social problems. In fact, maybe the best way to describe this approach is to say it uses the social psychologist's mind as its tool, a mind that has been trained to look at behavior in unique ways. The applied researcher takes as his or her topics not theoretical issues but questions about how to solve specific problems in a real, struggling, social world. The studies done by Lewin's CCI are a perfect example.

Still farther out on the applied continuum are social psychologists who have so devoted themselves to particular applied issues—such as organizational behavior, psychology of law, health psychology, and environmental psychology—that in many cases these specialties have become fields in their own right, spinoffs as it were from the mainstream of social psychology. (Interestingly, because issues of peace and social justice on the whole lack ready-made social institutions to support studies in the manner that medicine, law, and business fund research, these areas of concern have remained closer to the center of social psychology.)

Most social psychologists, however, keep one foot within social psychology proper, even as they explore the "real world." For example, they may offer themselves as consultants or advisers. Some even have private consulting practices in which they help individuals or organizations. Others tackle broad social problems, like child abuse or addictions. But they all tend to make important contributions just because of the perspective they bring to the problem. When Don Dutton began working with battered women's groups, for example, he was impressed by how well social psychology theory and methods had prepared him to be useful "out in the world."

Another example is Craig Haney. After conducting the Stanford prison study, Haney became dissatisfied with what he calls the "trickle down theory of social change"—that you do the research and it goes into journals and somehow gets where it needs to be. The Stanford study drew media attention and opened doors into government and the courts. But it was difficult to get their message across. Haney's solution was to learn more about law and the justice system, and he has made a career out of "making research results directly available to legislative agencies and organizations whose job it is to develop policy, making results have some kind of relevance to the constitutional questions the court is examining."

As a result, Haney has seen social psychology research on, for example, jury selection appear in places like California Supreme Court decisions. One decision, he says, "reads like a social science treatise. It changed the way juries are selected in California. That time the courts were really listening to what was being said."

Yet another example is Daryl Bem, the magician who developed self-perception theory as an alternative to cognitive dissonance theory. Like many social psychologists, Bem entered the field because he thought it was a way to help the world. Remember how he started out in physics at MIT? The social psychologist who changed Bem's mind was Thomas Pettigrew, who at nearby Harvard was teaching a course on race relations and had Freedom Riders up from the South to talk about the civil rights movement (and who has continued to be a central figure in the study of race relations). Pettigrew greatly renewed Bem's interest in social psychology and brought him, as Bem put it, "into the fold."

These days Daryl and his wife, Sandra Bem, are busy applying social psychology methods and ideas to a number of projects, in addition to continuing their more theoretical work. Opportunities come up particularly in her area, sex roles, in which she is one of the leading researchers. Daryl described several cases to us:

> We were asked by the Equal Employment Opportunity Commission to demonstrate that AT&T's advertising practices were perpetuating the segregation of jobs by always showing operators were female and linemen were men. We demonstrated the effect of that in a very simple study. And we won the case. We've done that three times in three different contexts. We consulted for the Highway Patrol in California—there are now women patrol officers. I have the feeling that it's the methods we apply that make the difference. But the results of the studies have the direct effects.

You recall Elliot Aronson, the former student of Leon Festinger who has earned a reputation as one of the outstanding experimentalists in the field. As a young assistant professor at Harvard, Aronson met one of the most senior members of the department, Gordon Allport. Allport had a strong sense of social commitment. For years, Aronson had always thought, as Festinger did, that it was enough to do the research and let someone else apply it. But he remembered Allport telling him that unless you apply the knowledge yourself, no one else will. That thought nagged Aronson, and so about fifteen years ago he substantially broadened the focus of his career.

He had been doing experimental work exclusively, on interpersonal attraction and self-esteem, at the University of Texas, when he became aware of problems in Austin's schools because of desegregation. In some schools, students of different races were staying particularly separate and hostile to each other. This situation tended to lower the self-esteem of the minority-race students, thus hurting their classroom performance and education (and their self-esteem still further)—hardly the intent of desegregation. When violence finally broke out, Aronson got involved and was permanently changed by the experience. He reports:

> My interet in self-esteem made it easy for me to jump into the school system when there was a crisis because of desegregation. But my actual involvement happened by accident. Austin was being desegregated and had riots. One of my former students was the assistant superintendent of schools for Austin, and he had heard me say many times in lectures how applicable this stuff is, so he thought of me to help solve this crisis. Then, once I'd tasted the experience of actually solving a crisis, Gordon Allport's influence became vivid. The laboratory seemed dull after that. Once we got significant results, instead of looking for another hypothesis to test in the laboratory, I was looking for another crisis to solve.

Essentially what Aronson did was apply the lesson from Robber's Cave. Do you remember what finally stopped the war between the Eagles and the Rattlers? A superordinate goal. Aronson decided that the goal for students is to learn. Thus he developed the "jigsaw classroom" (Aronson & Bridgeman, 1979), a method that forces students to cooperate in their learning.

Students meet in a six-person learning groups in which each has one part of the written lesson and teaches it to the others. For the group to get the whole lesson, all its members have to be allowed to present and everyone has to listen to everyone else, regardless of race or ethnic background. Evaluations of the program show that it greatly increases participation by those previously excluded, obviously, and also raises self-esteem, liking for school, positive inter- and intraethnic perceptions, and empathy. Members of minorities also get better grades.

While still an experimentalist, Aronson is now also involved in using social psychology knowledge about attitude change and social cognition to get socioeconomically lower households to make use of energy-efficient technology that is available for free but that up to now has not been adopted by most such households. And most recently he has begun a research project to evaluate the potential application of social psychology principles to making AIDS education more effective.

All in all, he feels the focus of his excitement has shifted from the *process* of research to its *outcome*, to the changes research can make in society:

> The whole idea for me now is to take research beyond the demonstration phase. Since 1971 I've spent a lot of my time in the office of school principals, trying to get them to understand why the jigsaw classroom would be useful in their schools—and failing more often than succeeding. I don't enjoy that process very much. But the beauty of jigsaw is not that it discovered something new. The beauty of jigsaw is that it packaged some knowledge in a way that works (the evaluations are superb) and that it is easy to use.

Another beauty of the jigsaw classroom for Aronson is the knowledge that it has made a difference in people's lives. He notes, "I still get letters from some of those kids in the classrooms, ones who are now in law school or in medical school, but who say they never would've gotten beyond the eighth grade if it hadn't been for that jigsaw experience."

As a result of his experiences applying social psychology, Aronson's viewpoint on social psychology's role in social change has altered markedly. Says he: "I obviously think it should be a lot stronger than it is now. There should be social psychologists in high-level positions in government."

He seems to be right, if you consider another example—Herbert Kelman—who is merely trying to use social psychology to maintain world peace.

Kelman told us he was excited by social psychology as an undergraduate and decided he wanted to study with Kurt Lewin when he heard him lecture at his college. But by the time Kelman was ready to enter graduate school, Lewin had died. Nevertheless, throughout his career Kelman has worked closely with many of those who studied with Lewin and has maintained an action-research perspective.

Kelman did his graduate work on attitudes, however, and is well known for his "functional theory of attitude change." Looking back, he thinks that this rigorous "pure science" work gave him enough prestige and credibility to go ahead and do what had always been most important to him: research that makes a difference in the world.

He was a major founder of the Research Exchange on the Prevention of War and of the *Journal of Conflict Resolution*, was instrumental in getting the Society for Psychological Study of Social Issues to set up a committee on international relations, and is widely known for a SPSSI-sponsored book he edited, *International Behavior: A Social Psychological Analysis*. Most inspiring is his ongoing work with international workshops on interactive problem-solving. He described them for us:

> The main idea is to provide an opportunity for people involved in a conflict to engage in the kind of interaction with each other that parties in a conflict usually can't engage in. Interaction in which they talk freely because the whole event is very, very private. Usually parties in conflict are talking for either their constituencies or third parties. They don't talk to each other, and what's even more important, they don't listen to each other.
>
> Essentially we try to get them to talk about the conflict analytically, rather than the typical blame-defend framework. . . . We don't minimize the significance of people's perception of their rights. But we try to get the parties to . . . express their own concerns, their basic needs and their basic fears, and to listen to the other's concerns—and then start asking questions about how can we find a solution that would be responsive to

> both sets of concerns simultaneously. That leads into a problem-solving stage.

Kelman has done most of his workshops with Palestinians and Israelis. Some have been with Egyptians and Israelis and with Greek and Turkish Cypriots. Notes Kelman:

> The whole effort here is designed not just as a learning experience for the participants but as a contribution to the larger political process.
>
> An example would be a workshop in which Palestinians come to the point where they can see that, for the Israelis, Zionism is a positive concept, that it is an expression of national liberation. They don't become Zionist. They still see it as inimical to their own interest. But they begin to understand that the meaning of Zionism isn't exhausted by the destruction of the Palestinians. And conversely, Israelis begin to understand what the PLO (Palestine Liberation Organization) means to the Palestinians. Again, they don't become supportive of the PLO. But they begin to see that the PLO is not just an agency dedicated to the destruction of Israel, but also a movement of national liberation and self-expression for the Palestinians. That Palestinians who identify with the PLO do so for positive reasons.
>
> This then leads to the next step. It is possible for an Israeli to be Zionist and for a Palestinian to be a supporter of the PLO and yet be interested in peace. In order to have peace, your enemy doesn't have to abandon his ideology, his commitment.

Mostly Kelman has worked with people who have influence in the decision-making process, sometimes even parliamentarians or party leaders (top leaders being, actually, poor candidates for the process because they "can't just toy with ideas . . . once they say something it becomes a political reality").

Although the conflicts he's worked on are still ongoing, Kelman knows some ideas that have come out of these workshops have reached decision makers and influenced their decisions. The changes have been small, but he sees an impact. And he finds personal satisfaction.

> I'm using everything that I am and that I have. Whatever knowledge and skills and experience and credibility I've built up over

> the years—I'm utilizing all of it in trying to make a contribution to the resolution of international conflict.

That seems to be a fairly concise description of a fulfilling career. Social psychologists seem to have a lot of such careers, perhaps because so many of them have devoted their lives to trying to help others while simultaneously using their minds to their utmost, with chutzpah and daring, in a cooperative (or playfully competitive) spirit with other bright, sociable people. Whether they choose to pursue pure research with the faith that deep knowledge best serves humankind or take their research out into the schools and social battlefields and find applications or use their minds as tools in applied settings—social psychologists generally show a deep concern for others.

In Conclusion: Science with Compassion

We asked Morton Deutsch to describe what kind of social psychology program he organized at Columbia Teachers College when he went there in 1963. His answer sums up this chapter very well:

> I wanted to create tough-minded but tender-hearted students . . . people that would be sharp and critical and would know theory and know research methods. . . . But I wanted them also to have a tender heart, to be concerned with social problems. . . . Science is very important. But science without a heart can be destructive. And a heart without a mind is not very valuable. So I think its very important to have both.

8

"We Are the World." *Social Psychologists Constantly Reflect on Themselves, Their Science, and Their World*

We have reached the last chapter. Looking back, you have met people, social psychologists by profession, who are caught up in the excitement of sorting out an issue, often very fine points of an issue, yet who tend to keep a very broad vision of their purpose. At their best, humans are like that—self-aware. They observe and reflect upon their personal and collective history and struggle to predict and improve on their behavior.

This is not to say that social psychologists are necessarily superior people or even more self-aware. But the paradigmatic social psychologist may be self-aware in a particularly useful way. A lot of people are saying today that if we as a species are going to make it into the next century, we are going to have to get control of ourselves as a group. Certainly no one wants a nuclear war or an environmental crisis, yet collectively we have somehow brought ourselves close to both. Somehow society influences us but we don't influence it. We need to figure that one out. And it is this that social psychologists are constantly thinking about: our impact on one another.

To understand our role in the world requires careful self-reflection. And it seems to us that this trait may be the one that most predominates within social psychology, at all the levels where we humans need to reflect—on ourselves as individuals, on our behaviors in groups, and on our role in our world. This chapter discusses the ways in which social psychologists are already engaged, to an unusual degree, in these three kinds of self-reflections.

When we started this book, we really didn't plan to end it this way; this chapter's topic was more or less shoved in front of us. You see, when we asked our fellow social psychologists what characteristics set social psychology apart from other areas of psychology or other social sciences, we often got the same kind of answer—social psychologists are more "self-questioning" of themselves and their field and the direction their society has taken. Let's begin to explore this characteristic at the personal level.

A Mirror Held Up to Themselves

Lots of kids grow up planning to become doctors, lawyers, teachers, bankers, and even physicists or biologists. By the time they enter college, some have even chosen to become rarer birds—entomologists or economists, for example. But how many kids have even heard of social psychology? Almost every social psychologist we spoke with did not enter college intending to become a social psychologist. Many did not even enter graduate school with social psychology on their mind. In this book we've seen that the field is populated by converts from English literature, physics, law, engineering, art, theology, chemistry, medicine—you name it. They also slipped in from other areas of psychology, ranging from clinical psychology to animal learning. All these people came into social psychology because they, unlike their fellow students who stayed in law school or seminary or what have you, started questioning themselves about what they were doing. Think back over them: Festinger and Bem both began in physics but liked the issues in social psychology better; Lewin began by studying general psychology, especially perception and learning; Heider slipped in from philosophy. At the outset of each person's career there was a sort of self-selection in favor of self-questioning.

Furthermore, while anyone may question his or her future plans, these people questioned *and* changed direction, making them also unusually flexible and perhaps even a bit impulsive and inclined to follow their hearts. As we have seen, a great many were looking for a place to express a deep-seated desire for doing something about the world. Others were excited about the enterprise of understanding human beings through scientific research. But it was rarely a drifting into social psychology; more often it was a self-reassessment. We especially enjoyed one story about this process, from Phil Zimbardo. He feels now that he was "practically born a social psychologist." But it took a fortuitous prod and some soul-searching for him to see it:

> [At Yale] I ran rats for three years. I was a rat man. The guy I was working for committed suicide. I applied for his grant. . . . I continued to do the research, even though originally I hated it. . . . Another graduate student and I did a study which was published in *Science*. . . . I was analyzing some of the data after it was accepted, running some other analyses. And Bob Cohen [a social psychologist doing work in dissonance theory] was sitting there. I guess I had had one course with him. And he asked me what I was doing. I got all excited describing the study—the effects of caffeine and chlorpromazene on the sexual behavior of the adult male rat. And he did a number on me. He said, "Could you look out the window and tell me what you see?"
>
> I thought he wanted me to see if his bike was there. I said, "I don't see anything." He [repeated the question]. . . . I said, "Well, there are some people."
>
> He started saying, "Well, what are they doing?"
>
> Again I kept thinking that they were people that he was waiting for. I started describing what they were doing. Then he just said something like, "Don't you think it would be more interesting to know what they were doing than to know what the rats are doing? Do you really care about the rats?"
>
> It was one of those things. At first I was offended and then later I thought about it. I said to myself, he's right—that's really why I'm here, that's what I was interested in when I started out—people. I'd put on my application that I was interested in race relations, and there I was, studying rats.

It is hard to say how broad this vein of self-reflection runs, for we were only asking those we interviewed about their career decisions. But we suspect they apply this type of questioning and analysis to themselves frequently, for some, at least, seem to allow themselves little ego-attachment to their projects. Remember the story of how Lewin showed up late at night at Cartwright's house with a new idea? The insight he'd come to discuss was one that meant "he would have to make a fundamental revision in his entire theoretical approach," and Cartwright still remembers "how surprised I was that anyone could be so pleased upon discovering a basic flaw in his own work" (Cartwright, 1978, p. 179).

Social psychologists seem to be constantly seeking new and more interesting, more significant, or just more fruitful approaches to their work. Or whole new topics. Schachter is famous for his broad range of topics—everything from emotions to smoking, affiliation to obesity. We saw that Bem was quite willing to agree to the validity of dissonance theory—after spending several years attacking it. Aronson switched from a highly theoretical career to a highly applied one. Festinger left social psychology altogether. Many, many major figures in social psychology have made dramatic changes in direction at several points in their careers. They look at what they are doing, they question, and they act on what they see.

A Mirror Held Up to Their Discipline

People in most professions would not publicly challenge the very assumptions of their discipline, but social psychologists do it constantly. Is our research relevant? Are we all wasting out time? Are we honest with ourselves? Are we throwing away the public's research funds? (You won't hear any other field ask *that* out loud. But social psychologists are well known among granting agencies for being harder on one another's grant proposals than members of any other area of psychology, sociology, or any other science. And *this* tendency, too, some social psychologists criticize. As Robert Zajonc said, "It is a very disturbing characteristic of this field. We have an unusual number of rejections in our journals, an unusual number of negative [peer] evaluations at foundations.")

The major psychology journals regularly publish articles by social psychologists raising questions about the fundamental value of what the field is trying to do or the way it is doing it. They are not just a few debunkers. Rather, they are the tip of the iceberg of an often-agonizing existential questioning of the worth of careers that many have spent most of their adult lives developing.

In the early 1970s, social psychology went through what is generally known as The Crisis. This period was an orgy of collective self-criticism, in which various authors argued that the "problem" with the field was that it was not applied enough. Or that it was not methodologically sophisticated enough. Or that it was too caught up in small, trivial studies and ignored the big questions. Or that it was constantly flitting from big question to big question without following up on the little details. People were having too much fun. Or not having enough fun. Or social psychology was too American, too individual-oriented, or too mechanistic. Or it was unethical in its research, or misguided in its attempts to be value-free and universal. And on and on and on.

Looking back at the history of the field, we see this crisis as an unusually strong example of what has been an ongoing process. Today, although the crisis has passed, many of those we interviewed expressed discouragement with where the field is now and where it seems to be going. These people were not only criticizing other people but feeling responsible themselves for the flaws they were eagerly cataloging.

What are the issues most in discussion these days? We heard three most often: the question of whether it is really possible to see beyond our cultural and historical context in order to discover general principles of human social life; the seeming split between social psychologists trained in psychology and those trained in sociology; and the influence of various social and economic forces on the field. Let's look at each.

The historical-context dispute, which has grown in prominence in recent years, strikes at the core of social psychology's identity as a science. While it may make sense for physics to seek unchanging laws of nature, social psychology deals with issues—racial prejudice, love, conformity, attitude change—that seem to be highly dependent on the particular culture and time. Furthermore, it makes no sense, some critics argue, to conduct research on modern North Americans and then claim to have found principles that apply to all cultures at all times. And it is not just a matter of studying more cultures or of studying back in time. The problem, some argue, is that *in principle* there are few regularities that hold true across cultures and times. Behavior—*all* behavior—is simply too embedded in its social and historical context.

This critique has been very much taken to heart by some. One social psychologist we interviewed called the argument "a knockout punch" for conventional social psychology. Thus a few social psychologists (such as Kenneth Gergen and Theodore Sarbin) have redirected their research to conceptualize it as "historical" or "contextual" social psychology, which attempts to understand our own social life in its particular context, without making claims for scientific universality.

The second concern of many social psychologists, that there are really *two* social psychologies, arises from the fact that while most of social psychology is conducted by people who are trained in university psychology departments and who then become professors in psychology departments, there is a numerically smaller but still substantial group of social psychologists who are trained and hired by sociology departments. George McCall, who refers to the two kinds as "PSPs" and "SSPs," explains that PSPs tend to focus on the individual—for example, the specifics of how the way the individual thinks, feels, or acts is affected by social influence. SSPs, in contrast, are more likely to focus on the social—for example, the nature of the social forces or social groups that produce the influences on the individual. Thus, research that focuses on how people perceive different social groups—such as research on the cognitive structure of social-class stereotypes—would be quintessentially PSP. But research that looked at how being in a particular social class affects the way people perceive different social groups would be pure SSP.

The two social psychologies tend to use different research methods. PSPs tend to favor the experiment, especially the laboratory experiment. SSPs tend to favor either the survey or the systematic analysis of experience. Of course, much social psychology research—for example, many of the classic studies on social influence—falls somewhere in between.

All this is fine and might even be very good if PSPs and SSPs were constantly learning from each other. But in fact, even when researchers from psychological and sociological backgrounds work on the same topic with the same methods, there are often considerable barriers to their knowing about and influencing each other's work. They are likely to attend and present papers at different conventions, read different scientific journals, teach courses from different textbooks, and have a different network of colleagues and associates. Even at the same university they might never even meet each other. And many social psychologists from both the psychology and the sociology sides told us they do not expect much change. Among some there is even a twinge of dislike for their colleagues across the PSP-SSP line. Obviously this boundary can be seen as a considerable obstacle to the efficient progress of social psychology.

Finally, many social psychologists expressed to us a concern about the social and economic forces that are impinging on social psychology today. The university system, the grant system, and the current demographics that have created a job shortage in social psychology have produced pressures that many see as working against creativity and the study of big questions. Several social psychologists we spoke with saw a creeping tendency toward "careerism"—social psychologists who see research as a way of making a living, rather than as an intrinsically rewarding activity.

On the brighter side, the first problem (of being bound to culture and time) is generally recognized as partially valid, but most social psychologists, particularly psychological social psychologists, see the critique as simply meaning that they must be more cautious about the claims they make—not that they must abandon their enterprise altogether. As David Myers notes, "Of course the discipline is value laden. But the way to go at that is not to make it more so." Or as Alice Eagley explains about this criticism:

> I agree with many of the points that they make—there is always bias in the position of the scientist. But I have a different view, in that I believe the scientific method builds in protections. We are striving for objectivity—and we are never going to reach the goal, of course, because of some of the things they point out. But every time we see bias, we try to build in protection. We've built in a lot already and we need to just keep doing it. We don't have to throw up our hands and say it is impossible.

As for the second problem, the two social psychologies, they are a definite reality, but some social psychologists are actively working to eliminate the split through interdisciplinary conferences, books, journals, research institutes, topical organizations, and even an occasional university department or research institute. For example, the close-relationships movement, which we described in chapter 3, is self-consciously interdisciplinary.

And as for careerism, the best news is that the job shortage should end and even reverse itself within the next few years. And while some "materialistic" tendency may exist, our interviews suggest that the field is in no danger of being overwhelmed by it. In the first place, nearly all the social psychologists we spoke with seemed so excited about their work that they would continue their research in a basement, if need be, and with no salary at all. In the second place, if money were the only issue, anyone bright enough and educated enough to be a social psychologist would have gotten a high-paying job in business long ago.

So, overall, while social psychologists continue to question themselves and one another, it is not a paralyzing self-criticism. Even the historical and contextual social psychologists are avidly pursuing research and theory within their approach. The SSPs and PSPs are not so worried about each other that they can't function. And careerism does not seem to have lessened the passion of the field as a whole.

Above all, this collective mauling seems to result in changes, and, remarkably enough given human behavior generally, often those who complained to us most vociferously about the state of the field were doing the most themselves to correct the problems they saw. For example, although some said the field had lost its spirit and excitement, when we asked these persons what projects in their career had been most satisfying, it was always their current one—or, as Robert Zajonc told us, "the one I'm about to do." Others said the field still was not doing enough about social problems. But these persons were actively pursuing research and action that was, indeed, making a real difference. Those who felt the field was too mechanistic (mainly the symbolic interactionists) were doing significant work showing social psychology how it could be nonmechanistic. And so on.

At the end of many of our interviews, we asked, "Over and above the other things you've talked about, is there anything you would want to tell someone about this field if he or she were considering entering it?" One said he'd ask, "have you considered art or music?" Others pointed out that the field is tough, and only those who are bright, creative, and self-motivated will find a comfortable home in it. Several stressed the value of getting a broad education—studying the natural sciences and humanities, reading Dostoyevski and Shakespeare. Many emphasized how important it is to love doing reserach.

But the main response was that this is a field like the American frontier: It offers unlimited opportunity, wide vistas, and a chance for any enterprising young man or woman to build an intellectual "empire." It is a field where new and radical ideas are unusually welcome, one where theories and methods of study can be borrowed from any field, from physics to drama.

What was even more striking about the answers to this question, however, was the readiness with which everyone could answer it. They had all obviously spent considerable time reflecting on the nature of the field and observing it as an outsider might. They were very able to stand back and verbalize what the field was, in its essence, to them. And they were eager to pass their observations and reflections on to anyone willing to listen.

A Mirror Held Up to the World

In closing, we must return to what we see as the essence of social psychology, its raison d'être—and that is what we discussed in chapter 2: While the rest of psychology—and the human race—has tended to think of humans as individuals, social psychology has studied the connection between individuals and social groups. It has recognized the existence of powerful if invisible social forces. And it has openly crusaded for a general recognition of those forces.

It is hard to appreciate what a breakthrough this realization could be for the human being's concept of itself as a species. Imagine what it must have been like for a one-celled animal when the first multicellular beasties were forming. Come on, imagine! You are all lining up in circles, passing food to one another, specializing a little bit, becoming interdependent. But you are all also probably thinking of yourselves as individuals—rugged ones, undoubtedly, if you have survived up to now.

Now imagine that one day the big evolutionary change comes and all of you stop seeing yourselves as individual organisms. You recognize that there is this group of you, and what you do affects the group, and what the group does affects you. You join the team. Why? Because you are surviving better as a multicellular animal than as a conglomerate of single cells.

At first you feel a bit diminished. Even threatened. What if the group chooses to go off and do something that endangers itself or your personally? So a bunch of you get together and get organized. You agree to have a few of you decide on policy and a few of those specialists will then let the whole group know when a change in policy has been made. (Lo, the first primitive nervous system.) Seeing that this change helps all of you survive even better, you get even more organized . . .

Today, humans may be evolving into a similar situation on this planet. Our global interdependence and communication among ourselves have grown so tremendously that we almost seem like one whole, in spite of our superficial divisions. Much depends now on our getting through that tricky period when the group moves off, almost randomly, and no one is in charge enough to say, "Hey, that's not a good idea for any of us." We need to develop some of us into social nervous systems, so to speak. And perhaps it is here that social psychologists fit into the picture.

As you have seen, social psychologists are acutely aware of the social reality—that they live within a larger whole—and many are constantly thinking about how they can give that whole a better knowledge of itself, how they can guide it better. In this book, whole chapters are devoted to these two facets of social psychology, seeing the reality of social forces and striving to improve their effects. All we are trying to add in this chapter is a little more perspective: When social psychologists reflect upon the social world, they may be leading us all toward an expanded awareness that will prove essential to our survival.

In Conclusion: It's Okay to Smile into the Mirror

You have seen in this book that social psychologists, although varied in personality and interests, often show a passion about their work that is perhaps surprising for a scientific discipline. They are not at all shy about taking on the major issues of the ages if that is what they enjoy. Their reality is social and cognitive, both personally and professionally, and they are on an active crusade to make that everyone's reality. Their research is an act of love, their theorizing is as exciting for them as an all-night student bull session, and they hope that their work will help build a better world.

In other words, besides all the serious social awareness in social psychology, these people seem to be having a lot of fun. Or at least getting awfully involved. We asked them about it. One of them, Jerry Singer, said it very eloquently: "Social psychology is what I enjoy."

When pushed, he added:

> I can't think of anything else I'd rather do. And people are willing to pay me handsomely for doing it. I can't believe that still. After all these years, when I shave every morning I think, "Today is the day they are going to find me out." Somebody is going to discover, "Hey, we've been paying him to do this."

We asked some social psychologists if they thought it was all right that it was so much fun. But the few times we got a serious answer, it seemed to us that the respondent hadn't understood the question. *Of course* it was all right to have fun, to be involved, to get excited. That's the *heart* of social psychology.

Of course, some will tell you that scientists are supposed to be dispassionate and dour. But Einstein certainly seemed to be enjoying himself. And Madame Curie was totally enthusiastic about chemistry and her wonderful radium. The Leakeys always seemed happiest around their digs. Jacques Cousteau is always beaming. Don't *all* scientists enjoy their work? Don't they all get worked up over their theories?

Yes, but would Roger Bacon, founder of the science-as-hard-objective-work school, approve?

There are some new answers to all of that, thanks to the reflection of science upon itself through fields called the psychology and sociology of science. In particular, we have enjoyed the ideas of I.J. Mitroff (1974) (a social psychologist, of course), who has written a book entitled *The Subjective Side of Science*, based on his study of NASA lunar scientists. Mitroff concludes that all the best scientists whom he studied were very subjectively involved in their work. Further, Mitroff insists that they had to be if they were going to stick it out through all the boring periods and setbacks that arise during a major research project.

Yet these individual, subjective scientists still produce objective scientific knowledge—through the social structure of science. That is, the facts get distilled from all this subjectivity by the larger scientific community. While each scientist may not be able to be entirely objective about his or her own corner of the field, it is still possible for each to be objective about other people's work, when it is close to but outside of his or her own. Thus, with time, the wheat gets separated from the chaff and the truth separated from the polemics, just as we saw in the cognitive dissonance versus self-perception theory dispute. And the good work gets done because it was fun and exciting to do, not methodical and dull. Or as Mitroff says,

> For too long one of the myths we have lived with is that science is a passionless enterprise performed by passionless men, and

> that it *has* to be if it is to be objective. What this myth ignores is that many of the great scientific achievements of the past have been the result of passionate, if not outright biased, inquiries. . . . [S]cience is no less objective because of this passion. Indeed, there are serious reasons for contending that science is more, not less, objective *precisely because of* (and not in spite of) the presence of great passions. (1974, pp. 23—24)

Therefore, if social psychology is more passionate and fun than most other sciences, it is certainly not more so than good science in any field, at least according to Mitroff. Perhaps, as with its self-reflection and social awareness, it is merely blazing the trail through certain murky spots it best understands.

We would like to close with the words of one of social psychology's founders, Muzafer Sherif:

> I disagree completely with those that say that science is aloof, that science should be a cool thing, without emotion. I don't think that there is anybody who has produced anything creative, any Nobel Prize winners in any fields, who haven't felt personally excited about their work, or who haven't been concerned about human beings.
>
> [Social psychology] isn't a job that you go to from nine to five and then quit and forget about it. For me social psychology . . . is value-charged. . . . People in the human sciences . . . should be . . . purely concerned about it . . . not learn psychology like a little trade and do our little technical things and carry on little social activities. The human sciences . . . should develop a keen consciousness of the situation. And then feel to do something about it . . . not . . . because we have to make a living . . . but [because we are concerned] about the predicament we humans are in today.

References

Allport, G.W. (1968). The historical background of modern social psychology. In G. Lindzey & E. Aronson (Eds.), *The handbook of social psychology* (Vol. I, 2nd ed., pp. 1–80). Reading, Mass.: Addison-Wesley.

Aron, A. (1970). Relationship variables in human heterosexual attraction. Unpublished doctoral dissertation, University of Toronto.

Aron, A. (1988). The matching hypothesis reconsidered again: Comments on Kalick and Hamilton. *Journal of Personality and Social Psychology, 54,*441–46.

Aron, A., & Aron, E.N. (1981). Experimental interventions of high coherence groups into disorderly social systems. Paper presented at the annual convention of the American Psychological Association, August, Los Angeles.

Aronson, E. (1980). Persuasion via self-justification: Large commitments for small rewards. In L. Festinger (Ed.), *Retrospections on social psychology* (pp. 3–21). New York: Oxford University Press.

Aronson E., & Bridgeman, D. (1979). Jigsaw groups and the desegregated classroom: In pursuit of common goals. *Personality and Social Psychology Bulletin, 5,* 438–66.

Aronson, E., & Carlsmith, J.M. (1963). Effect of the severity of threat on the devaluation of forbidden behavior. *Journal of Abnormal and Social Psychology, 66,* 584–88.

Aronson, E., & Mills, J. (1959). The effect of severity of initiation on liking for a group. *Journal of Abnormal and Social Psychology, 59,* 177–81.

Asch, S.E. (1946). Forming impressions of personality. *Journal of Abnormal and Social Psychology, 41,* 258–90.

Asch, S.E. (1958). Effects of group pressure upon the modification and distortion of judgments. In E.E. Maccoby, T.M. Newcomb, & E.L. Hartley (Eds.), *Readings in social psychology* (3rd ed., pp. 174–83). New York: Holt, Rinehart & Winston.

Asch, S.E. (1959). A perspective on social psychology. In S. Kock (Ed.), *Psychology: A study of a science* (Vol. 3, pp. 363–83). New York: McGraw-Hill.

Back, K.W. (1972). *Beyond words: The story of sensitivity training and encounter groups.* New York: Russell Sage Foundation.

Bales, R.F. (1950). *Interaction process analysis: A method for the study of small groups.* Cambridge, Mass.: Addison-Wesley.

Bales, R.F. (1958). Task roles and social roles in problem-solving groups. In E.E. Maccoby, T.M. Newcomb, & E.L. Hartley (Eds.), *Readings in social psychology* (3rd ed., pp. 437–47). New York: Holt, Rinehart & Winston.

Bales, R.F., & Slater, P.E. (1955). Role differentiation in small decision-making groups. In T. Parsons & R.F. Bales (Eds.), *Family, socialization, and interaction process* (pp. 259–306). Glencoe, Ill.: The Free Press.

Baumrind, D. (1964). Some thoughts on ethics of research: After reading Milgram's "Behavioral study of obedience." *American Psychologist, 19,* 421–23.

Bem, D.J. (1965). An experimental analysis of self-persuasion. *Journal of Experimental Social Psychology, 1,* 199–218.

Bem, D.J. (1967a). Self-perception: An alternative interpretation of cognitive dissonance phenomena. *Psychological Review, 74,* 183–200.

Bem, D.J. (1967b). Reply to Judson Mills. *Psychological Review, 74,* 536–37.

Bem, D.J. (1972). Self-perception theory. In L. Berkowitz (Ed.), *Advances in experimental social psychology* (Vol. 6, pp. 1–62). New York: Academic Press.

Brickman, P., Coates, D., & Janoff-Bulman, R. (1978). Lottery winners and accident victims: Is happiness relative? *Journal of Personality and Social Psychology, 36,* 917–27.

Cartwright, D. (1978). Theory and practice. *Journal of Social Issues, 34,* 168–80.

Cartwright, D. (1979). Contemporary social psychology in historical perspective. *Social Psychology Quarterly, 42,* 82–93.

Cohen, D. (1977). *Psychologists on psychology.* New York: Taplinger.

Cooley, C.H. (1902). *Human nature and the social order.* New York: Scribner.

Crutchfield, R.S. (1955). Conformity and character. *American Psychologist, 10,* 191–98.

Darley, J.M., & Gross, P.H. (1983). A hypothesis-confirming bias in labeling effects. *Journal of Personality and Social Psychology, 44,* 20–33.

Deutsch, M., & Collins, M.E. (1951). *Interracial housing: A psychological evaluation of a social experiment.* Minneapolis: University of Minnesota Press.

Dillbeck, M.C., Landrith, G., & Orme-Johnson, D.W. (1981). The transcendental meditation program and crime rate change in a sample of forty-eight cities. *Journal of Crime and Justice, 4,* 25–46.

Donnerstein, E.I., & Berkowitz, L. (1981). Victim reactions in aggressive erotic films as a factor in violence against women. *Journal of Personality and Social Psychology, 41,* 710–24.

Duck, S. (1988). Introduction. *Handbook of personal relationships: Theory, research, and interventions.* New York: Wiley.

Dutton, D.G., & Aron, A.P. (1974). Some evidence for heightened sexual attraction under conditions of high anxiety. *Journal of Personality and Social Psychology, 30,* 510–17.

Ehrlich, D., Guttman, I., Schonbach, P., & Mills, J. (1957). Post-decision exposure to relevant information. *Journal of Abnormal and Social Psychology, 54,* 98–102.

Evans, R.I. (1976). *The making of psychology: Discussions with creative contributors.* New York: Knopf.

Evans, R.I. (1980). *The making of social psychology.* New York: Gardner Press.

Fazio, R.H., Zanna, M.P., & Cooper, J. (1977). Dissonance and self-perception: An integrative view of each theory's proper domain of application. *Journal of Experimental Social Psychology, 13,* 464–79.

Festinger, L. (1954). A theory of social comparison processes. *Human Relations, 7,* 117–40.

Festinger, L. (1957). *A theory of cognitive dissonance.* Stanford, Calif.: Stanford University Press.

Festinger, L., & Carlsmith, J.M. (1959). Cognitive consequences of forced compliance. *Journal of Abnormal and Social Psychology, 58,* 203–10.

Finison, L.J., (1979). An aspect of the early history of the Society for the Psychological Study of Social Issues: Psychologists and labor. *Journal of the History of the Behavioral Sciences, 15,* 29–37.

Geiwitz, J., & Moursund, J. (1979). *Approaches to personality.* Monterey, Calif.: Brooks/Cole.

Glass, D.C., & Singer, J.E. (1972). *Urban stress: Experiments on noise and social stressors.* New York: Academic Press.

Gottman, J.M. (1979). *Marital interaction.* New York: Academic Press.

Greenwald, A.G., & Ronis, D.L. (1978). Twenty years of cognitive dissonance: Case study of the evolution of a theory. *Psychological Review, 85,* 53–57.

Haney, C., Banks, C., & Zimbardo, P.G. (1973). Interpersonal dynamics in a simulated prison. *International Journal of Criminology and Penology, 1,* 69–97.

Hazen, C., & Shaver, P. (1987). Romantic love conceptualized as an attachment process. *Journal of Personality and Social Psychology, 52,* 511–24.

Heider, F. (1958). *The psychology of interpersonal relations.* New York: Wiley.

Heider, F. (1983). *The life of a psychologist.* Lawrence: University Press of Kansas.

Heider, F., & Simmel, M. (1944). An experimental study of apparent behavior. *American Journal of Psychology, 577,* 243–59.

Hilgard, E.R. (1987). *Psychology in America: A historical survey.* San Diego, Calif.: Harcourt Brace Jovanovich.

Janis, I.L. (1972). *Victims of groupthink.* Boston: Houghton Mifflin.

Jones, E.E., & Davis, K.E. (1965). From acts to dispositions: The attribution process in person perception. In L. Berkowitz (Ed.), *Advances in experimental social psychology* (Vol. 2, pp. 219–66). New York: Academic Press.

Jones, R.A, Linder, D.E., Kiesler, C.A., Zanna, M., & Brehm, J.W. (1968). Internal states or external stimuli: Observers' attitude judgments and the dissonance theory–self-persuasion controversy. *Journal of Experimental Social Psychology, 4,* 247–69.

Kalick, S.M., & Hamilton, T.E. (1986). The matching hypothesis reexamined. *Journal of Personality and Social Psychology, 51,* 673–82.

Kelley, H.H. (1950). The warm-cold variable in first impressions of persons. *Journal of Personality, 18,* 431–39.

Kelley, H.H. (1967). Attribution theory in social psychology. In D. Levine (Ed.), *Nebraska Symposium on Motivation,* 1967 (Vol. 15, pp. 192–240). Lincoln: University of Nebraska Press.

Kelley, H.H., & Thibaut, J.W. (1954). Experimental studies in group problem solving and process. In G. Lindzey (Ed.), *Handbook of social psychology* (Vol. 2, pp. 735–85). Cambridge, Mass.: Addison-Wesley.

Kelley H.H., & Thibaut, J.W. (1978). *Interpersonal relations: A theory of interdependence.* New York: Wiley-Interscience.

Krech, D. (1975). David Krech. In G. Lindzey (Ed.), *A history of psychology in autobiography* (Vol. 6, pp. 219–50). Englewood Cliffs, N.J.: Prentice Hall.

Krech, D., Crutchfield, R.S., & Ballachey, E.L. (1962). *Individual in society: A textbook of social psychology* (3rd ed.). New York: McGraw-Hill.

LaFrance, M., & Mayo, C. (1976). Racial differences in gaze behavior during conversations: Two systematic observational studies. *Journal of Personality and Social Psychology, 33,* 547–52.

Lamberth, J. (1980). *Social psychology.* New York: Macmillan.

Langer, E.J., & Rodin, J. (1976). The effects of choice and enhanced personal responsibility for the aged: A field experiment in an institutional setting. *Journal of Personality and Social Psychology, 34,* 191–98.

Latane, B., & Darley, J. (1970). *The unresponsive bystander: Why doesn't he help?* New York: Appleton-Century-Crofts.

Latane, B., Williams, K., & Harkins, S. (1979). Many hands make light work: The causes and consequences of social loafing. *Journal of Personality and Social Psychology, 37,* 822–32.

Lewin, G. (1948). Preface. In D.C. Cartwright (Ed.), *Field theory in social science: Selected theoretical papers by Kurt Lewin* (pp. vii–xiv). New York: Harper & Brothers.

Lewin, K. (1939). Experiments in social space. *Harvard Educational Review, 9,* 21–32.

Lewin, K. (1948). *Resolving social conflicts.* New York: Harper.

Lewin, K. (1951a). Field theory and learning. In D.C. Cartwright (Ed.), *Field theory in social science: Selected theoretical papers by Kurt Lewin* (pp. 60–86). New York: Harper & Brothers. (Reprinted from *Yearbook of the National Society for the Study of Education, 1942, Part II,* pp. 215–42.)

Lewin, K. (1951b). Problems of research in social psychology. In D.C. Cartwright (ed.), *Field theory in social science: Selected theoretical papers by Kurt Lewin* (pp. 155–69). New York: Harper & Brothers.

Lewin, K., Lippitt, R., & White, R.K. (1939). Patterns of aggressive behavior in experimentally created "social climates." *Journal of Social Psychology, 10,* 271–99.

Leyens, J-P., Camino, L., Parke, R.D., & Berkowitz, L. (1975). Effects of movie violence on aggression in a field setting as a function of group dominance and cohesion. *Journal of Personality and Social Psychology, 32,* 346–60.

Lippitt, R., & White, R.K. (1947). An experimental study of leadership and group life. In T.M. Newcomb and E.L. Hartley (Eds.), *Readings in social psychology* New York: Holt, Rinehart & Winston.

Locksley, A., Ortiz, V., & Hepburn, C. (1980). Social categorization and discriminatory behavior: Extinguishing the minimal intergroup discrimination effect. *Journal of Personality and Social Psychology, 39,* 773–83.

McKillip, J., & Riedel, S.L. (1983). External validity of matching on physical attractiveness for same and opposite sex couples. *Journal of Applied Social Psychology, 13,* 328–37.

MacKinnon, D.W. (1949). Introductory remarks (Kurt Lewin Memorial Award Meeting). *Journal of Social Issues, 5,* Supplement Series 3, 3–4.

Markman, H.J., Floyd, F.J., Stanley, S.M., & Storaasli, R.D. (1988). Prevention of marital distress: A longitudinal investigation. *Journal of Consulting and Clinical Psychology, 56,* 210–17.

Marrow, A.J. (1969). *The practical theorist.* New York: Basic Books.

Mehrabian, A., & Ferris, S.R. (1967). Inference of attitudes from nonverbal communication in two channels. *Journal of Consulting Psychology, 32,* 248–52.

Milgram, S. (1963). Behavioral study of obedience. *Journal of Abnormal and Social Psychology, 67,* 371–78.

Milgram, S. (1964). Issues in the study of obedience: A reply to Baumrind. *American Psychologists, 19,* 848–52.

Miller, G.R., & Burgoon, J.K. (1982). Factors affecting assessments of witness credibility. In N.L. Kerr & R.M. Bray (Eds.), *The psychology of the courtroom* (pp. 169–94). New York: Academic Press.

Mills, J. (1967). Comment on Bem's "Self-perception: An alternative interpretation of cognitive dissonance phenomena." *Psychological Review, 74,* 535.

Mitroff, I.J. (1974). *The subjective side of science.* New York: Elsevier.

Murphy, G. (1965). The future of social psychology in historical perspective. In O. Klineberg & R. Christie (Eds.), *Perspectives in social psychology* (pp. 21–34). New York: Holt, Rinehart & Winston.

Myers, D.G. (1982). Polarizing effects of social interaction. In H. Brandstatter, J.H. Davis, & G. Stocker-Kreichgauer (Eds.), *Group decision making* (pp. 125–61). New York: Academic Press.

Newcomb, T.M. (1947). Autistic hostility and social reality. *Human Relations, 1,* 69–86.

Newcomb, T.M. (1958). Attitude development as a function of reference groups. In E.E. Maccoby, T.M. Newcomb, & E.L. Hartley (Eds.), *Readings in social psychology* (3rd ed., pp. 265–75). New York: Holt, Rinehart & Winston.

Newcomb, T.M. (1974). Theodore M. Newcomb. In G. Lindzey (Ed.), *A history of psychology in autobiography* (Vol. 6, pp. 365–91). Englewood Cliffs, N.J.: Prentice Hall.

Phillips, D.P. (1983). The impact of mass media violence on U.S. homicides. *American Sociological Review, 48,* 1150–74.

Phillips, D.P. (1986). Natural experiments on the effects of mass media violence on fatal aggression: Strengths and weaknesses of a new approach. In L. Berkowitz (Ed.), *Advances in Experimental Social Psychology* (Vol. 19, pp. 207–50). Orlando, Fla.: Academic Press.

Rodin, J., & Langer, E.J. (1977). Long-term effects of control-relevant intervention with the institutionalized aged. *Journal of Personality and Social Psychology, 35,* 897–902.

Rogers, C.R. (1968). Interpersonal relationships, USA. *Journal of Applied Behavioral Science, 4,* 265–80.

Rosenthal, R., & Fode, K.L. (1963). The effect of experimenter bias on the performance of the albino rat. *Behavioral Science, 8,* 183–89.

Rosenthal, R., & Jacobson, L.F. (1968). Teacher expectations for the disadvantaged. *Scientific American, 218,* 19–23.

Ross, L.D., Amabile, T.M., & Steinmetz, J.L. (1977). Social roles, social control and biases in social-perception processes. *Journal of Personality and Social Psychology, 35,* 485–94.

Rubin, Z. (1970). Measurement of romantic love. *The Journal of Personality and Social Psychology, 10,* 265–73.

Schachter, S. (1959). *The psychology of affiliation.* Stanford, Calif.: Stanford University Press.

Schachter, S., & Singer, J. (1962). Cognitive, social, and physiological determinants of emotional state. *Psychological Review, 69,* 379–99.

Schultz, D. (1975). *A history of modern psychology* (2nd ed.). New York: Academic Press.

Sears, D.O., & Abeles, R.P. (1969). Attitudes and opinions. In P.H. Mussen and M.R. Rosenzweig (Eds.), *Annual Review of Psychology* (Vol. 20, pp. 253–88). Palo Alto, Calif.: Annual Reviews.

Sherif, M. (1935). A study of some social factors in perception. *Archives of Psychology, 27,* No. 187, 1–60.

Sherif, M. (1966). *In common predicament: Social psychology of intergroup conflict and cooperation.* Boston: Houghton Mifflin.

Sherif, M., Harvey, O.J., White, B.J., Hood, W.E., & Sherif, C.W. (1961). *Intergroup conflict and cooperation: The Robber's Cave experiment.* Norman: University of Oklahoma Book Exchange.

Sherif, M., & Sherif, C.W. (1969). *Social psychology.* New York: Harper & Row.

Slater, P.E. (1955). Role differentiation in small groups. In A.P. Hare, E.F. Borgatta, & R.F. Bales (Eds.), *Small groups: Studies in social interaction* (pp. 498–515). New York: Knopf.

Snyder, M., Tanke, E.D., & Berscheid, E. (1977). Social perception and interpersonal behavior: The self-fulfilling nature of social stereotypes. *Journal of Personality and Social Psychology, 35,* 656–66.

Strickland, L.H., Aboud, F.E., & Gergen, K.J. (1976). The "power structure" in social psychology. In *Social psychology in transition* (pp. 307–16). New York: Plenum.

Tesser, A. (1978). Self-generated attitude change. In L. Berkowitz (Ed.), *Advances in experimental social psychology* (Vol. II, pp. 289–338). New York: Academic Press.

Thibaut, J.W., & Kelley, H.H. (1959). *The social psychology of groups.* New York: Wiley.

Tolman, E.C. (1948). Kurt Lewin—1890–1947. *Journal of Social Issues, 4,* 22–26.

Triplett, N. (1898). The dynamogenic factors in pacemaking and competition. *American Journal of Psychology, 9,* 507–33.

Tuddenham, R.D., & Macbride, P. (1959). The yielding experiment from the subject's point of view. *Journal of Personality, 27,* 259–71.

Valins, S. (1966). Cognitive effects of false heart-rate feedback. *Journal of Personality and Social Psychology, 4,* 400–408.

Walster, E., Aronson, V., Abrahams, D., & Rottman, L. (1966). Importance of physical attractiveness in dating behavior. *Journal of Personality and Social Psychology, 4,* 508–16.

Watson, J.B. (1913). Psychology as the behaviorist views it. *Psychological Review, 20,* 158–77.

Wayenbaum, I. (1907). *La physinomie humaine: Son mecanisme et son role social.* Paris: Alcan.

Wheeler, L., Reis, H.T., & Nezlek, J. (1983). Loneliness, social interaction, and sex roles. *Journal of Personality and Social Psychology, 45,* 943–53.

White, G.L., Fishbein, S., & Rutstein, J. (1981). Passionate love and the misattribution of arousal. *Journal of Personality and Social Psychology, 41,* 56–62.

White, G.L., & Kight, T.D. (1984). Misattributions of arousal and attraction: Effects of salience of explanations for arousal. *Journal of Experimental Social Psychology, 20,* 55–64.

Zajonc, R.B. (1980). Cognition and social cognition: A historical perspective. In L. Festinger (Ed.), *Retrospections on social psychology* (pp. 180–204). New York: Oxford University Press.

Zajonc, R.B. (1985). Emotion and facial efference. *Science, 228,* 15–21.

Zuckerman, M., DePaulo, B.M., & Rosenthal, R. (1981). Verbal and nonverbal communication of deception. *Journal of Personality and Social Psychology, 43,* 347–57.

Index

About the Authors

ARTHUR ARON earned his B.A. in psychology and philosophy in 1967 and his M.A. in psychology in 1968, both at the University of California, Berkeley, and his Ph.D. in psychology in 1970 at the University of Toronto. His dissertation included one of the first experimental studies of romantic attraction and led to a program of research that has continued to be influential in social psychology. After receiving his doctorate, he held positions at the University of British Columbia, the University of Paris (Laboratoire de Psychologie Sociale), Maharishi International University, the Institute for Advanced Research, California Graduate School of Family Psychology, and Santa Clara University, among others. He is currently teaching at the University of California, Santa Cruz.

ELAINE N. ARON earned her B.A. in psychology in 1968, Phi Beta Kappa, from the University of California, Berkeley, and her M.A. in psychology in 1970 from York University. She has subsequently held a variety of positions in counseling and the training of counselors, university teaching, and research. For the past few years she has spent most of her time engaged in independent research and writing and has had eight books published, ranging from scholarly treatises on her research to a historical novel.

Together the Arons have published or presented at scientific meetings more than a hundred papers on their research, which has focused on a variety of topics, including creativity, the social effects of meditation, social change, emotions, and group processes. Currently, their main interest is in examining the implications of a theory of motivation within close relationships, a topic they developed in a recent book, *Love and the Expansion of Self: Understanding Attraction and Satisfaction.*